A STRAIGHTFORWARD
GUIDE
TO
THE RIGHTS OF THE
CONSUMER

David Bryan

Editor Roger Sproston

Straightforward Guides
www.straightforwardco.co.uk

Straightforward Guides

978-1-913342-84-5

Printed by 4edge www.4edge.co.uk

Cover design by BW Studio Derby

A Straightforward Guide to the Rights of the Consumer

CONTENTS

Introduction

****

INTRODUCTION

The aim of this Guide, updated to **January 2021**, is to outline the rights of the consumer when entering into a transaction with a seller of goods, whatever those goods might be. People do not know their rights when encountering problems at the point of sale or after. What, for example, are your rights if goods turn out to be unsuitable or substandard and the seller refuses to let you have your money back or generally tells you that there is nothing that can be done?

There are three legal systems in the United Kingdom: English Law, which covers Wales as well, Scottish law and Northern Irish law. In practice there is very little difference between English law and Northern Irish law so reference throughout this book will be to English law. Scottish law differs significantly. Courts have different procedures and some laws are different. There will be a brief resume of Scottish law in chapter 17.

BREXIT- Key points to consider in relation to consumer law:
European law and regulations may well change in the future following BREXIT (final withdrawal) in January 2021. To ensure that there is a smooth transition The Consumer Protection (Amendment etc.) (EU Exit) Regulations 2018 have been passed. This instrument:
a) makes amendments to EU derived consumer protection legislation which are necessary as a result of the decision to leave the European Union. This is to ensure that the legislation continues to operate effectively at the point the United Kingdom withdraws

from the European Union; b) revokes the EU Online Dispute Resolution Regulation; c) makes amendments to EU derived consumer protection legislation to replace obsolete cross-references to EU law. These out-dated references were in place before the decision to leave the European Union and correcting them now ensures that the law will function properly after exit day.

The Law Society has published guidance for solicitors that highlights the changes in consumer law including civil and commercial cooperation that will occur should the UK leave the EU without having reached an agreement with the EU. In this scenario, the EU and UK will have failed to sign a withdrawal agreement (governing the terms of the UK's departure from the EU) and an agreement governing the future relationship between the two parties. The UK will immediately leave the EU's institutional structures without a transition period. In many areas, cooperation between the UK and EU will cease, and the applicable legal regime in many practice areas will change.

UK-based organisations that provide for alternative dispute resolution (ADR) will no longer act in cross-border disputes between the UK and EU/EEA states. Instead, consumers will need to engage ADR entities in the country in which the retailer is based.

The European Commission's Online Dispute Resolution (ODR) procedure will no longer be available to UK consumers.

The European Small Claims procedure will no longer be made available to UK consumers. Additionally, UK consumers will not be able to pursue a claim in the UK small claims court where the retailer is based in an EU/EEA state.

The European Health Insurance Card will no longer be made available to UK residents/citizens. This means that those travelling from the UK to EU/EEA states will need to purchase health insurance to cover accidents and emergencies following a no-deal Brexit.

Any judgment of a UK court made against an EU/EEA retailer will no longer be automatically enforceable against the retailer in that country. Instead, UK-based consumers may need to employ a lawyer in the country where the retailer is based to enforce their rights. They may alternatively launch proceedings directly in the country concerned.

BREXIT and the effect on consumer law is discussed further in Chapter 16, Consumer Issues Generally.

COVID 19 and Consumer rights

2020 has been quite a tumultuous year for everyone and peoples consumer rights have been impacted in almost all areas, particularly travel.

Covid-19 has filled our hospitals, shut down our workplaces and transformed how we live – but it hasn't changed our fundamental consumer rights.

Across the country, consumers have had gigs, flights and weddings cancelled. They have struggled to return faulty goods because the shops are closed, they have had emails about refunds ignored and they have been left in financial limbo as their rights seem to be disregarded.

While the COVID-19 crisis does not bring changes to consumer protection rules, it does bring them into sharper focus and regulators will be quick to act against any blatant breaches. Consumer rights have not changed and people still have important legal protections. Of course, most businesses are trying to do the right thing in a really difficult time, while they also deal with the pressures of the pandemic. Some may be overwhelmed by customer demands at a time when they are also short-staffed.

But if you are going to enforce your rights then you need to know what they are and how Covid-19 might be affecting how quickly they can be resolved.

Refunding travel costs

This is a widespread issue for would-be holidaymakers across the world. The situation concerning UK travellers will be discussed further on in this book. People with travel booked for 2021 face tremendous uncertainty as they wait to find out if their holidays will be cancelled or otherwise. Those with travel plans cancelled in 2020 are still waiting for refunds, often being fobbed off with vouchers or the offer of a postponement.

If your holiday has been cancelled then you are entitled to a refund. However, the consumer champion Which? has found that 10 of the UK's biggest package holiday providers and 10 of the largest airlines are failing to refund customers in the statutory timeframe of 14 days after you request it.

Of course, it may be a struggle for providers to refund everyone immediately and many customers will be happy to accept their break being rescheduled. If you are happy to accept a new holiday or a credit note then make sure it comes with Atol protection so your money is not at risk if the provider goes under.

If you are not happy to do so then put your request for a refund in writing and keep pestering the provider until your consumer rights are met. We will discuss this further in chapter 14.

Weddings being delayed-Refunds and Insurance

Many couples were looking forward to spring or summer 2020 for their weddings and now have had to delay their big day to 2021. But many face distressing financial consequences as well.

A number of wedding insurers say their policies do not cover weddings being cancelled for this kind of reason, leaving couples without the financial protection they thought they had.

Once again, your rights do not change just because the world has. If you have read your policy carefully and believe that it should cover this kind of event (many have quite limited cover) then the first step must be a formal complaint to the insurer themselves.

If that is rejected then the next step is a complaint to the Financial Ombudsman. It is free to make a complaint and they will investigate on your behalf. If they find in your favour then they can order the insurer to pay you.

The Financial Ombudsman service is under pressure, as you'd expect, and its website warns that at busy times it can take around four months to assign new cases to a handler.

Not everyone has wedding insurance, and many people want their money back from the suppliers and venues they had booked.

While many businesses are doing what they can to help couples postpone their events, some are refusing refunds or demanding additional payments.

The Competition and Markets Authority (CMA) has put out additional guidance to businesses, including highlighting that it expects in most cases a full refund would be paid if a business has cancelled a contract without providing any of the goods or services as a result of the current lockdown.

If you've been affected by unfair cancellation terms, you can report the businesses involved to the CMA using its online form.

Childcare provision

This has been a very difficult time for nurseries and childminders, many of which struggle to make ends meet even without a lockdown. As a result, some have continued to charge parents for childcare even when the children were unable to attend because of the lockdown rules.

Many childcare contracts do specify that parents must continue paying even if their child is unable to attend, although the majority have not done so during this crisis.

However, for parents whose childcare settings are still billing, the CMA has said it expects refunds to be paid when "no service is provided by a business, for example because this is prevented by the restrictions that apply during the current lockdown". Again, there is the opportunity to highlight unfair treatment to the CMA through its website.

Returning faulty items–problems because of the lockdown

Many retailers have agreed to longer returns periods as a result of the lockdown(s) as they know that it may be harder for customers to enforce their rights. If you are shopping online then make sure you find out first what the returns policy is so you know what your rights are.

If you want to return an item or reject a service then it's important to understand your rights to do so. If the current lockdown makes it harder to enforce your rights then it is a sensible idea to email the company.

That way there is a record that you intended to complain or return an item within the accepted timeframe but were prevented from doing so.

The current situation doesn't mean you have fewer rights but it may mean you have to fight harder to reinforce them.

General points

A main area which causes problems, and is always in the news, is that of consumer credit. The Government has put forward various White Papers which seek to impose a greater regulatory framework on all areas of consumer credit as it is feared that individual borrowing is reaching unacceptable levels. Payday loans (a legal form of loan sharking) are the latest area of lending to undergo scrutiny and subsequent action. In 2018, the most high profile payday loan company, WONGA, went into administration, focussing attention in the area. In 2021 expect more to follow. However, as will be explained in the chapter on consumer credit, Payday loan firms are now back again, some flouting the law, taking advantage of people who have suffered during lockdown and may have lost their jobs. Same old story although the government hopefully will be taking much needed action.

Hire agreements are also covered along with the sale of unsafe goods. Food safety and general hygiene are also outlined. Holidays and travel firms generally are covered, particularly with the problems caused by the pandemic. In addition, there is a section that covers general consumer issues such as dealing with banks, mobile phones, dry cleaning, travel insurance and private sales. Finally, there is a section on saving for Christmas, outlining pro's and cons's of the safest ways to save.

Updates to the rights of tenants when renting, in particular the ban on lettings agents fees and other charges to tenants, plus COVID related rules are also included in chapter 2. Finally, there are ten top tips for dealing with online scams which are becoming ever more prevalent.

Data Protection Act 2018

The Data Protection Act 2018 is a United Kingdom Act of Parliament which updates data protection laws in the UK. It is a national law which complements the European Union's General Data Protection Regulation and updates the Data Protection Act 1998. This Act greatly strengthens the rights of consumers.

The Consumer Rights Act 2015

The Consumer Rights Act came fully into effect on 1st October 2015. The legislation introduced new consumer rights and remedies when purchasing digital content (such as video games and digital music), as well as building upon what constitutes an unfair contract term when dealing with consumers. It replaced the then existing legislation under the Sale of Goods Act 1979 and Supply of Goods and Services Act, to the extent of dealing with consumers for the sale of goods and supply of services. The Act also replaced the Unfair terms in Consumer Contracts Regulations.

A consumer for the purposes of the 2015 legislation is defined as "an individual acting for purposes that are wholly or mainly outside that individual's trade, business, craft or profession".

The Act is underpinned by the Consumer Contracts (Information, Cancellation and Additional Charges) Regulations 2013 (the **Regulations**) which came into force on 13 June 2014 (replacing the Consumer Protection (Distance Selling) Regulations 2000 (for contracts made after June 2014) and the Cancellation of Contracts Made in a Consumer's Home or Place of Work Regulations 2008 (albeit these latter provisions still apply to contracts made before 13 June 2014). Also, the Consumer Rights (Payment Surcharges) Regulations 2012 (the **Surcharges Regulations 2012**) were introduced which came into force on 6th April 2013. These regulations are covered in chapter 7 and chapter 8 respectively. Updates to all areas are included.

****

Chapter 1

Consumer Protection Generally

Consumers are protected by both civil and criminal law. As we shall see below, the general law of contract gives some protection, especially from misrepresentation. There are special rules for consumer contracts, including:

- Contracts for buying goods
- Contracts for services
- Distance selling
- Other areas such as package holidays, insurance, food and finance

The tort of negligence gives limited protection where the consumer has no contractual rights. In addition, there is protection from defective goods under the Consumer Protection Act 1987. The criminal law also affords some protection against such matters as trade descriptions.

The law of contract
All transactions between consumers and suppliers are based on the law of contract. Every exchange of goods is an agreement between buyer and seller. It therefore follows that underlying each exchange is an area of law which defines the rights and obligations of both

buyer and seller. The purchaser and the person who sells goods and services are not free to do exactly as they wish after the sale or, indeed, make up the rules as they go along. The major area of law which supports consumers from October 1st 2015, is the Consumer Rights Act. It should be noted that the *Supply of Goods (Implied Terms) Act 1973* will cover business to business contracts and consumer to consumer contracts only.

Sale of Goods Act 1979/ Sale and Supply of Goods Act 1994 will still apply to business to business contracts and to consumer to consumer contracts.

Supply of Goods and Services Act 1982 will cover business to business contracts and consumer to consumer contracts only.

Unfair Contract Terms Act 1977 will cover business to business and consumer to consumer contracts only.

The below is a summary of the Act and how it now protects consumers in respect of goods and services and also digital content, including free digital content.

The Consumer Rights Act 2015-Goods

Under the Consumer Rights Act 2015, all goods supplied under a consumer contract should:

- be of satisfactory quality;
- be fit for purpose;
- match the description, sample or model; and
- be installed correctly (if part of the contract).

Rights of a consumer to return goods Under the CRA 2015

There is an Initial rights to reject the goods – an automatic 30 day period to return the goods if they do not meet the implied terms unless the expected life of the goods is shorter than 30 days. This right entitles the consumer to a 100% refund.

Right to repair or replacement - If the 30-day period has lapsed or during that time, the consumer chooses not to exercise their right to reject goods, they will be entitled in the first instance to claim a repair or replacement. This remedy will be deemed a failure if, after one attempt at repair or replacement, the goods still do not meet the necessary requirements.

Right to a price reduction and final right to reject - If repair or replacement is unavailable or unsuccessful to the consumer, then they can claim a price reduction or a final right to reject the goods. The reduction or refund can be up to 100% of the product value.

Significant exclusions

Consumer rights are subject to the following exclusions:

- before contract, where defects are brought to the consumer's attention, or if the consumer examines the goods and any defects should have been obvious;
- where a consumer changes his/her mind about wanting the goods;
- if the product was used for a purpose that is neither obvious nor made known to the trader; or

- where faults have appeared as a result of fair wear and tear (only applicable 6 months after the goods are provided to the consumer).

Services

Like the implied terms that exist currently under Supply of Goods and Services Act, the services must be performed to a certain standard. Under the Consumer Rights Act, all services supplied under a consumer contract should:

- be carried out with reasonable care and skill;
- completed for a reasonable price (where no price is specified, i.e. hourly rates);
- completed within a reasonable time (where no timescale is provided); and
- completed in accordance with any information said or conveyed in writing to the consumer where the consumer relies on it (intended to include quotations, assurances regarding timescales and information provided pre-contract to the customer which induces them to purchase services from the trader). This is in addition to any rights that may arise as a result of a misrepresentation.

Rights of a consumer when services do not comply

Repeat performance of the services - when a provider fails to exercise reasonable care and skill or where requirement arising from information they gave about the service is breached. This cannot be used where it would be impossible to finish providing service to the required standard.

Reduction of price - A price reduction can also be claimed where the service is not provided within a reasonable time; or the supplier breaches the terms given to consumers, whether orally or in writing regarding the standards of service. Can be up to 100% of agreed price.

Appointment of new supplier. Only in circumstances where getting the original supplier to do the work is impracticable or unreasonable, the consumer may have a claim for remedial work by another supplier.

Significant exclusions

Consumer rights are subject to the following exclusions:

- where unless agreed to the contrary, it does not achieve the consumer's desired outcome (provided trader uses reasonable care and skill);
- where it is the consumer who is responsible for things going wrong (supplier should always make notes of instructions);
- where damage is caused by the consumer.
- where the consumer simply changes their mind ; or
- where faults have appeared as a result of fair wear and tear.

Consumers have additional rights where contracts are subject to Consumer Contracts (Information, Cancellation and Additional Charges) Regulations 2013, for example under a distance/off-premises contract. These are explained further on in the book.

Digital content

The Consumer Rights Act definition of digital content is: "data which [is] produced and supplied in digital form.

Any physical media that hosts digital content (such as a CD or Blu-ray) carrying faulty content is still subject to the Consumer Rights Act relating to goods, but content on that item will be governed by the digital content provisions of the Consumer Rights Act.

Under the Consumer Rights Act, digital content must be:

- of satisfactory quality (taking into account description of the content, the price paid and other circumstances such as labelling and advertising);
- fit for a particular purpose; and
- as described (including system requirements and another other information given to the original digital content). Upgrades can add to this description.

Most computer operating systems or games have minor bugs that are corrected over time with patches or upgrades and this will be tested objectively as what is "reasonable" to be deemed acceptable in the context of satisfactory quality.

Significant exclusions

Consumer rights are subject to the following exclusions:

- the consumer's attention was drawn to an unsatisfactory aspect of the digital content before a contract was made (for example if a game is in beta testing where bugs are typically accepted as part of the game);

- where the consumer examines the digital content before the contract is made and that examination ought to reveal the unsatisfactory aspect; or
- where a trial version is examined by the consumer before the contract is made and a reasonable examination of the trial product ought to make the unsatisfactory aspect apparent (for example, watermarks on files produced by the product).

Remedies under the Consumer Rights Act for defective digital content

Repair or replacement - the consumer does not have a choice of repair or replacement if it is either impossible to do so or disproportionate compared to another available remedy. If content is defective within six months of its supply, it is to be taken as being defective on the day it was supplied.

Price reduction - this is only triggered if the remedy of repair/replacement is not possible or where it has been requested and not provided within a reasonable time. The remedy may be up to the full cost of the digital content.

Data Protection Act 2018

In May 2018, the General Data Protection Regulation (GDPR) came into force across the EU. The UK passed the Data Protection Act 2018 that complements the GDPR with some additional provisions for domestic law. Some of the key changes include: Online identifiers, such as your IP address, will count as personal data. Your consent will need to be active and clear, meaning when you agree to be contacted you'll have to tick a box that makes it clear about what you're agreeing to You'll be able to make a subject access request free of charge A company must delete your data when you ask it to – unless there's a compelling reason to keep it Compensation can now be claimed from a processor rather than only the data controller. It's important to note that GDPR adds to, rather than alters or reduces, consumer rights and protections.

Other remedies
The following remedies can be claimed either in addition to, or instead of the remedies above:

- a claim for damages;
- forcing the supplier to perform the contract;
- a full refund; or
- not to pay for the product.

It should be noted that a consumer can never recover the same loss twice.

"Free" content
The Consumer Rights Act enables a consumer to be able to rely on the remedies provided for faulty or damaging 'free' digital content. For the consumer to be able to do this the digital content must be supplied under a contract where the consumer has to pay for goods, services or other digital content – computer magazines, for

example, typically provide a 'free' CD with various software included with the magazine.

Damage to devices

- Where digital content causes damage to a device or to other digital content (such as corrupting files), and that device or content belongs to the customer and the damage is a kind of which would not have occurred if the supplier had exercised reasonable skill, then one of the following remedies will be available to the consumer:
- repair of the damage, which must be done within a reasonable time, without significant inconvenience and without cost to the consumer; or
- payment of compensation, which must be given without undue delay, and in any event within 14 days of the trader agreeing to pay the compensation. The trader cannot charge the consumer a fee for this.

Unfair terms

The Consumer Rights Act 2015 replaces and adds to the current rules on unfair terms in consumer contracts under Unfair Contracts Terms Act 1977 ("UCTA") and Unfair Terms in Consumer Contracts Regulations 1999 ("UTCCR") in respect of consumer contracts. An unfair term of a consumer contract is not binding on the consumer, and the assessment of whether a term is unfair will continue to be based on whether the term under scrutiny causes a significant imbalance in the parties' rights and obligations under the contract, to the detriment of the consumer.

Whether a term is fair (or unfair) is to be determined by taking into account:

- the nature of the subject matter of the contract (i.e. the circumstances of the contract);
- reference to all the circumstances existing when the term was agreed; and
- to all of the other terms of the contract or of any other contract on which it depends.

The Consumer Rights Act will apply to consumer notices (whether contractual/non-contractual, oral or written) as well as consumer contracts in the typical form.

What constitutes fairness?
In deciding whether a term in a contract is fair or fair, the term in question will be subject to a "fairness test". The fairness test will be used to decide whether a particular term (or terms) is fair or unfair however, in respect of terms relating to contract price and/or subject matter itself, the fairness test will only be considered in respect of the to the extent that such terms are not "transparent and prominent", for example, if they were hidden away in small print. This ensures that the Consumer Rights Act is not a tool for challenging the price or the essence of a contract.

In addition to the terms above, under the Unfair Terms in Consumer Contracts Regulations , there is currently a list of terms which may be regarded as unfair; known as a "grey list". A term being listed on the "grey list" means that it is assessable for fairness even if the term is "transparent" and/or "prominent".

In addition to the existing grey list terms, the Consumer Rights Act 2015 adds three additional terms to the grey list:

- a term which has the object or effect of requiring that, where the consumer decides not to conclude or perform the contract, the consumer must pay the trader a disproportionately high sum in compensation or for services which have not been supplied. (including a "termination fee" for cancellation of a contract);
- a term which has the object or effect of permitting the trader to determine the characteristics of the subject matter of the contract after the consumer has become bound by it; and
- a term which has the object or effect of giving the trader the discretion to decide the price payable under the contract after the consumer has become bound by it, where no price or method of determining the price is agreed when the consumer becomes bound.

Restrictions on excluding liability

Although the Consumer Rights Act 2015 is not intended to prevent businesses from limiting liability in their entirety, businesses looking to include in their terms and conditions limitations should note the following:

- it is not possible to exclude or limit the application of the remedies for faulty goods and digital content (such as right to repair or replacement) that are implied into all consumer contracts under the Consumer Rights Act; the implied term that the services will be provided with reasonable skill and care cannot be excluded or limited for the reasons above; andwhilst it is possible to limit liability for supply of services in respect of price and time for performance (provided that such a limit will not prevent the consumer from being able to recover the full contract price), any other limitations in respect of service performance would be subject to a test of fairness.

****

Chapter 2

The Consumer Rights Act 2015 and Letting Agents

Letting agents — display of fees

The British Government set out its approach to banning letting fees in England in The Tenants Fees Act 2019 (effective from 1st June 2019). Lettings fees are already banned in Scotland and in Wales from September 1st 2019.

In summary:

All payments are prohibited except rent, deposits and three exceptions. Landlords or their agents will no longer be allowed to charge tenants for anything except: the rent, the tenancy deposit and a holding deposit (more on these below).

This means they will no longer be allowed to ask tenants to cover the cost of their own referencing. They also won't be able to charge check-in, inventory or admin fees.

Three Fees Are Exempt

The only three exceptions are for contract amendments and two kinds of 'default' fees. These are fees they can charge when the tenant breaks the tenancy agreement. Landlords will have to write these clauses into the tenancy to be able to charge tenants these fees while the tenancy is in progress.

(a) Late Rent Fees

Landlords will be able to charge fees for rent payments that are over 2 weeks late. The fees can be up to 3% plus the Bank of England base interest rate. Because this is an annual interest rate, landlords will have to calculate the amount of pro rata interest accrued on the outstanding rent.

(b) Lost Keys

Landlords will also still be able to charge tenants for losing their keys (or other security device if your property is high-tech). But they will only be able to charge a reasonable amount for which they can provide evidence of the cost to them.

Remember, both default fees will need to be included in the tenancy agreement for the landlord to be able to charge them, and previous rules about fair clauses will still apply.

(c) Changes to Tenancy

Landlords can charge up to £50 for making changes to the terms of the tenancy. For example, adding a new tenant to the tenancy or allowing a pet. A Landlord can charge more than £50 if they are able to demonstrate their costs exceeded £50, but it is expected that this will not happen often.

Crucially, this exception **does not apply** to renewals or changes to the length of the tenancy.

3. Cap on Tenancy Deposits

Tenancy deposits, also called security deposits, are limited to five weeks' rent for annuals rents under £50,000. For properties whose annual rent is £50,000 or more, tenancy deposits will be capped at six weeks' rent. Holding deposits are limited to one weeks rent.

5. New Rules on Holding Deposits
The Act includes new rules about how holding deposits must be treated. The holding deposit must be returned to the tenant: either in payment back to the tenant, or being put towards the first rental payment, or the security deposit.

There are some exceptions. In these cases the landlord can keep the holding deposits:
- If The tenant withdraws
- The tenant doesn't take all reasonable steps to enter the tenancy
- The tenant fails a right to rent check
- The tenant provides misleading information which materially affects their suitability to rent the property

6. Repayment of Holding Deposits
Landlords will only be able to hold the holding deposit for 15 days unless another 'deadline' date is agreed in writing. After the deadline, the holding deposit must be repaid within 7 days according to the above rules. The holding deposit can be repaid to the tenant, or it can be put towards the rent or tenancy deposit.

What Are the Penalties to Landlords Who Charge Tenant Fees?
Landlord (or agents) who charge illegal fees face paying huge fines. The first offence would be a civil offence, with a fine of £5,000. If

the offence is repeated within five years, there would be either a criminal offence or a fine of £30,000. There are also plans to help tenants recoup any illegal fees they paid from the landlord (or agent). Local Trading Standards organisations will enforce the ban.

It will require Trading Standards to enforce the ban and to make provision for tenants to be able to recover unlawfully charged fees and a lead enforcement authority will be appointed in the lettings sector. There is an amendment to the Consumer Rights Act 2015 to specify that the letting agent transparency requirements should apply to property portals such as Rightmove and Zoopla.

The 2015 Consumer Rights Act
One of the first new provisions brought into force by the passing of the Consumer Rights Act 2015 relates to requirements for accommodation letting agents and property management businesses to display their fees and charges to clients. As we have discussed above, the fees are now regulated by law. The requirements relate to businesses that receive instructions from clients regarding accommodation to be let under assured tenancy agreements to:

- introduce prospective tenants to landlords with available accommodation for rent
- arrange assured tenancy contracts between landlords and tenants
- carry out property management services for landlords

- The fees that have to be indicated are the fees, charges and penalties payable to the letting agent by their clients under contracts for:
- introducing tenants to landlords with available accommodation for rent
- arranging assured tenancy agreements
- the management of rental properties
- However, the following fees do not have to be indicated:
- rental charges
- tenancy deposits
- any fees, charges, penalties that the letting agent receives from a landlord under a tenancy on behalf of another person
- any other fees, charges or penalties specified in regulations

An assured tenancy is one as defined in the Housing Act 1988 (excluding long leases as defined in the Leasehold Reform, Housing and Urban Development Act 1993) except where the landlord is a:

- private registered provider of social housing
- registered social landlord
- fully mutual housing association

Display requirements

Letting agents must display a list of relevant fees in each of their premises where they deal with clients or potential clients face-to-face, on their website, where applicable. This list must be displayed in a conspicuous place.

Fees content

The displayed fees list must include:

- an adequate description of each fee and its purpose
- whether the fee is payable for the accommodation or by each tenant
- the total amount of the fee inclusive of all taxes
- the method of calculating the fee, if the fee cannot be determined in advance

In England only, letting agents engaging in letting agency or property management work relating to private accommodation must also display the following:

- a statement regarding whether the business is a member of a client money protection scheme
- a statement that they are a member of a redress scheme and the name of that scheme, where applicable

Penalties

A penalty of up to £5,000 can be imposed by trading standards services for breaches of these requirements, subject to any statutory guidance issued and an appeals procedure.

****

Chapter 3

Faulty Goods/Non-Receipt of Goods

When it comes to faulty goods many consumers are unaware of the protection and statutory rights they are legally entitled to. The situation, as outlined in the introduction concerning the Coronavirus pandemic has made things worse. Shops often exploit their customers' uncertainty and violate shoppers' statutory rights by shirking their legal responsibility to remedy situations by offering refunds, repairs or replacements.

Under the Consumer Rights Act 2015, traders are legally responsible to sell goods which are:

- 'as described', meaning the the actual product must match any description(s) given to the customer before purchase by which the goods are identified
- of satisfactory quality, that is they are of a standard that would reasonably be expected taking into consideration the price paid and description. In appropriate circumstances the quality of the goods will include freedom from minor defects, durability, safety, and appearance and finish.
- fit for all purposes made known to the seller at the time of purchase
- The Act states that if goods turn out to not fulfill any of these criteria you have the right to demand a refund from the seller

- unless you have accepted the goods. The act provides that goods have been 'accepted' by the buyer where:
- you tell the seller you have accepted them
- you do something to or with them which prevents you from giving the goods back in their original state, such as alter, consume or damage them
- you keep the goods for 30 days without rejecting them

It is a good idea to report the problem to the seller as soon as you become aware of the fault. If you do wish to reject the goods you must give clear notice of this to the seller. If you allow 30 days to elapse then you no longer have the right to a refund, but you are still entitled to get the item repaired or replaced for free instead. Faulty goods are also often covered by the manufacturer's guarantee or warranty, but this is in addition to your automatic rights retailer. Your rights may also extend beyond the manufacturer's guarantee once it has expired.

How to obtain refunds for faulty goods
If a fault develops soon after you purchased an item, or if it was faulty straight away, meaning the goods are not of satisfactory quality, then you are entitled to a full refund from the retailer. The legal term to use here is the 'right to reject' under the Consumer Rights Act 2015 as the item was not of satisfactory quality. You must give the seller clear notice that the item is rejected within 30 days for a refund to be given. To obtain a refund:

- Contact the retailer. Tell them you want to reject the item and would like a full refund. If the item is genuinely faulty and 30 days have not elapsed since the purchase, you should get a refund. You will probably need to provide proof of purchase but remember this doesn't always have to be a receipt. It can be a credit card or bank statement, a witness, a cheque stub or any other evidence that proves you bought the product from that retailer. If the retailer rejects your claim then check to see if the faulty goods are covered by the manufacturer's guarantee. If they are then tell the manufacturer about the fault and ask for a refund.

- If neither the retailer nor manufacturer offers a refund then write to the retailer again formally rejecting the faulty goods under the Consumer Rights Act 2015. Explain that you will take the matter to the small claims court unless a full refund is offered.

- If the retailer still does not offer a refund then after this then you may want to consider getting the item replaced or repaired instead. If, however, you are adamant that you want a refund, you may be able to take the case to the small claims court.

- If you paid for the faulty goods with a credit card and they cost between £100 and £30,000, the creditor card company will be jointly liable with the seller if the goods are not of satisfactory quality and you are entitled to a refund from either the seller or your credit card provider under Section 75 of the Consumer Credit Act. You can also use this method if the retailer goes out of business after you buy the faulty goods.

How to get faulty goods repaired or replaced

Under the Consumer Rights Act 2015, your rights may allow you to get faulty goods repaired or replaced for free up to six years after purchase (five years in Scotland), although the longer you have had the goods the progressively more difficult it will be to show the defect arose as a result of the state of the goods at time of purchase.

If the fault arises within six months of the purchase, and it's not because of fair wear and tear, accidental damage or misuse, then the retailer must repair or replace the faulty goods. If the retailer objects, he must prove that the item wasn't faulty to begin with or that it wasn't expected to last very long.

If six months have passed and something goes wrong, you might still get a repair or replacement but you will have to prove that the goods were inherently faulty, i.e. show that there is no other cause, such as accidental damage, for the fault. To help you prove this, you may wish to obtain and independent expert's report to back up your claim, although these can be expensive. To get faulty goods repaired or replaced:

- Contact the retailer, tell them about the problem and ask for the goods to be either repaired or be replaced. You can specify which you'd prefer but it is ultimately a question of what is more economical from the perspective of the retailer.
- You will probably need to provide proof of purchase but remember this doesn't always have to be a receipt. It can be a credit card or bank statement, a witness, a cheque stub or any

other evidence that proves you bought the product from that retailer.

- Alternatively, if the faulty goods are still covered by their guarantee, contact the manufacturer, tell them about the problem and ask for the goods to be repaired or replaced.
- If the retailer or manufacturer do not help, write to the retailer and make a more formal request. Say that you are exercising your rights under the Consumer Rights Act 2015 as the item is not of "satisfactory quality" and you would like to have it repaired or replaced.
- In your letter, warn the retailer that if it fails to accept to your demands you will start proceedings in the small claims track of the County Court.
- If your retailer still refuses to cooperate then consult our guide to taking a dispute to the County Court and consider taking that route. Bear in mind that you cannot take a case to court if you purchased the faulty goods more than six years ago.

Second-hand goods and sale items

The Consumer Rights Act 2015 also covers goods bought second hand, as well as goods bought at a discount price in a sale. However the requirement that goods be of satisfactory quality does not apply to a particular defect where:

- that particular defect has been pointed out to you before you agreed to buy the goods, and/or
- you inspect the goods before agreeing to buy them and the particular defect is one that you should really have spotted.

The Consumer Protection Act 1987

An additional form of consumer protection is contained in the Consumer Protection Act 1987, which relates to the physical protection of the consumer and his/her property from the effects of faulty or defective products. A product is defective under the 1987 Act if it is not as safe as the average person would be entitled to expect.

Whether you buy or hire goods, they have to be safe. If you are injured by them in any way as a result of their hazardous nature, then the manufacturer and the importer (if it has come from outside the EU) are strictly liable for any damage or loss caused to you or those that used the product.

"Strict liability" means that you do not have to prove that they were at fault. What you will have to prove is that the product was defective, and that it was this defect that caused the injury, or in tragic cases, even death. Therefore, if you are injured when your car, whether it is your own, hired or being bought on HP, crashes due to a defect then you could sue the manufacturer for your injury and losses. However the Act only applies to damage caused to goods other than those that are defective, it does not allow you to claim for the cost of the defective goods themselves only the damage or injury caused to other goods or people by the defect.

Non receipt of goods and late delivery-Delivery rights

The retailer is responsible for goods until they are in your physical possession or in the possession of someone appointed by you to accept them.

This means that retailers are liable for the service provided by the couriers they employ - the delivery firm is not liable.

The retailer is responsible for the goods until they are delivered to you and in your possession.

Late deliveries

There is a default delivery period of 30 days during which the retailer needs to deliver unless a longer period has been agreed. If the retailer fails to deliver within the 30 days or on the date that has been agreed, you can do the following:

- If your delivery is later than agreed and it was essential that it was delivered on time, then you have the right to terminate the purchase and get a full refund.
- If the delivery isn't time essential but another reasonable delivery time can't be agreed, you're also within your right to cancel the order for a full refund.

****

Chapter 4

Other Consumer Transactions

In chapter three we looked at the law and faulty goods, transactions between seller and buyer which are covered by the Consumer Rights Act 2015. However, there are transactions which are not covered by the Act, simply because there is no "transfer of property for a monetary consideration called a price".

An example may be the purchase of a good under a hire purchase agreement. We will be discussing this in more depth later. However, purchase of goods in this way constitutes "bailment". In other words, the goods are owned by the hire purchase company until the last payment is made. If the good is defective in this case, what is the remedy? Hire purchase transactions of this kind are covered by the Consumer Rights Act 2015.

There is another form of consumer transaction which needs to be understood. This is known as the *conditional sale transaction.* This is where a buyer of a good, a typical example being a car, may have the car for six months and have constant trouble. If the buyer experiences ongoing trouble and the garage is alerted then he will be entitled to a refund of his money.

There is an important point to be made here. That is the buyers attitude and whether or not he accepts the good even though it is defective. Two notions exist - acceptance and affirmation. What this means is that acceptance will occur when the buyer accepts delivery. However, affirmation can only occur when the defect is known, with time starting to run from that point. If the buyer simply carries on driving the car, or using the good even though there is knowledge of the defect then he is accepting the good and undermining his right to return or seek compensation. However, if the buyer does not affirm, i.e., continually lets the garage know that there has been problems, then he is not affirming the contract and will be entitled to a refund.

Be very careful here. Always assert your right, do not be afraid of complaining and keep a record of the number of times that you have complained.

Use of materials when carrying out repairs

Responsibility, or liability, for parts under a contract which is for works and materials is regulated by the Supply of Goods and Services Act 1982. If a remedy is needed for the supply of parts which are either defective or are not those which are supposed to have been used then it is to this Act that you must turn. As before, the notion of affirmation and acceptance is of paramount importance.

When it comes to the service element of a contract, as opposed to the materials element, then it is to The Supply of Goods and Services that you must turn. Section 13 states that work must be carried out with reasonable care and skill.

There is one famous legal case which tends to set the standard in this area. This case was Bolam v Friern Hospital in 1957. This involved the medical profession and the issue was deciding whether a doctor is liable for negligence and comparisons with a so-called "average doctor". The connection here is that if you are complaining about standards of work then you would need to demonstrate that the average garage could have carried out the work to a higher standard.   There are other terms implied into a service contract. Section 14 implies that the business doing the servicing must carry it out within a reasonable time. This is where there are no express terms in the agreement. Section 15 indicates that where no price has been agreed then a reasonable price must be agreed. A reasonable price is one which another company would charge for the same work. Therefore, if you feel that you are being overcharged then you can challenge it, underpinned by the backing of section 15 of this Act.   There is one very important rider here. That is if the supplier has quoted a high price and the consumer has accepted then there can be no redress, not even if you find that another company will provide that service for far less.

CONSUMER BEWARE. Always shop around. If you feel that the price is too high then ask elsewhere. Always try to avoid entering into an agreement with no stated price.

Of course, there will always be the case where it is not really possible to get a price. This is where protection under section 15 comes in.

EXAMPLE
You discover that you are receiving electric shocks off your car. You telephone a local garage that specialises in car electric's and the

41

owner tells you to "drop your car in". You do this and telephone the garage later to see what the problem is. The garage owner informs you that the problem was minor, with a power lead earthing. The problem has been rectified and you can collect the car. You do this and you are informed that the bill is £150. Quite rightly, you think that this is too high. Two things can happen here, and often do. On one hand the garage owner can tell you that that is what he charges and you must pay it. The other is that you can find out what an alternative garage would pay for the same work and establish a reasonable price, refusing to go above this.

The problem that you have to sort out here is how to get your car back. You have to argue the case with the garage and let them know that you understand your rights as a consumer and you have read and understood the law that governs this particular problem.

It is the case that when businesses realise that they may get bad publicity and the person in front of them knows their rights, they generally back down, as it is bad for business. If there has been a breach of services contract then the normal solution or remedy is damages to put the defective or poor work right. Damages for distress or disappointment can be awarded in some cases although there are certain areas where it is difficult, such as holidays.

The Consumer Protection Act 1987

The above Act covers those instances where a person has been injured because of a defective good. This Act also covers the many instances where someone may have been injured or affected who is not the principal purchaser but has been injured.

The Consumer Protection Act therefore imposes a very strict liability for defective goods on someone who is deemed to be the producer of the product. The Act provides, or at least seeks to provide, a route for the consumer to seek redress against the person who is ultimately responsible for the damage. This gets rid, or at least minimises the requirement to have to prove fault, which in the past has proven very time consuming and difficult and also very expensive.

The Act is only relevant where the consumer has purchased a defective product which has caused damage. It is essential to determine who is liable, and the Act says that the following are primarily liable for damages:

a) the producer
b) an own brander who has held himself to be the producer of a particular good
c) the first importer into the European Community. Therefore, strict liability will attach to any person or company who presents its/his self as producer of a good.

Only in a few cases will the supplier of a good be liable. These cases are limited to instances where it may not be possible to identify the producer or anyone else within or further up the chain, in a reasonable period of time.

It is necessary to define product. This is because some goods and services are more readily identifiable than others as products. Section 1(2) of the Act defines product and has wide definitions. For example, goods include electricity. Section 45 also defines goods produced from the land, such as crops, and other goods such as aircraft vehicles etc. A product, however, is a common sense notion and for the purposes of the every day consumer a product is fairly obvious.

A defective product is simply where the safety of the product is in question and can be a manufacturing defect, a design defect and a defect that has arisen because of a misleading warning notice. In this latter instance, this means a notice that has failed to advise the consumer how to use a product properly. A consumer can sue under the Consumer Protection Act (s5) for:

- Death caused as a result of a defective product
- Personal injury caused as a result of a defective product
- Damage to private property, above a certain sum, caused as a result of a defective product.

The is no liability for any damage to the product itself or for the loss of, or any damage to, the whole or any part of any product which has been supplied with a product. There are cases where, even if a manufacturer is liable under the Act, the Act contains what is known as strict liability and not absolute liability. This means that there are a number of defences that can be used by manufacturers. It is up to the defendant, i.e., the manufacturer to prove one of the following as a defence:

- The defect was caused by the need to comply with the law as it stands at that time. This may have been the need to comply with new legislation that has recently been introduced

- The manufacturer did not supply the product in question-this can relate to instances of theft
- That the supplier of the good is not in business and is a private individual. Remember, the aim of the Act is to impose strict liability on commercial producers and it is not really the intention, or the spirit of the Act to impose any liability on individuals as such. However, individuals who are not in business are not ruled out.
- That the defect did not exist in the product at the time of supply. One very good example has been the recent spate of contaminating certain products as they lay on shelves, such a baby food and also chocolate. If contamination takes place in the shop then it is important to note that the seller, or retailer becomes liable under the Sale of Goods Act.

Another defence, perhaps the most complicated and controversial is that of the state of scientific (and technical) knowledge at the time was not such that a producer of products of the same description as the product in question might be expected to have discovered. Here, a producer of a product has to demonstrate that at the time in question they could not be expected to know of the defect. Finally, that the producer of a component part of a product had produced a defective product and the defect was as a result of instructions given by the main producer. A consumer may bring a claim against a manufacturer within a certain timescale - in relation to personal injuries or any damage to property there is a three year time period within which to bring a claim. However, as far as a manufacturer of a product is concerned, there is a 10-year cut off point from the time that a particular product was supplied to a retailer. There are some instances where a recall notice may be issued by a manufacturer to a retailer. This is happening all the time, in the cases of bay food, cars and other items. This in no way relieves the manufacturer of liability although it can certainly help to reduce the amount of compensation gained by an aggrieved person.

****

.

Chapter 5

Guarantees and Warranties

Guarantees and Warranties

In law, a guarantee is an agreement given by a trader to a consumer, without any extra charge, to repair, replace or refund on goods which do not meet the specifications set out in the guarantee. A warranty is an insurance policy which provides cover for the unexpected failure or breakdown of goods, usually after the manufacturer's or trader's guarantee has run out.

Guarantees and warranties are additional to the legal rights you have as a consumer and must not affect those rights in any way.

What is a guarantee?

In law, The Consumer Rights Act 2015, a guarantee is an agreement given by a trader to a consumer, without any extra charge, to repair, replace or refund goods that do not meet the specifications set out in the guarantee. A guarantee is usually issued by the manufacturer of goods or by a trader that provides goods as part of a service - replacement windows, for instance. Generally, a guarantee provider undertakes to carry out free repairs, for a set period of time, for problems that can be attributed to manufacturing defects.

An insurance backed guarantee provides the consumer with protection if the trader that provided the goods or service under theguarantee ceases to trade and can no longer fulfil its obligations under the guarantee. The insurance company underwrites the terms of the guarantee for the remainder of the guarantee period. A guarantee is additional to the legal rights you have as a consumer and must not affect those rights in any way.

What is a warranty?

A warranty (or extended warranty) is broadly defined in law as a contract for cover for goods, which is entered into by a consumer for (money) monetary consideration.

A warranty is a form of insurance policy which provides cover for the unexpected failure or breakdown of goods, usually after the manufacturer's or trader's guarantee has run out. Some warranties are service contracts rather than insurance backed (you should check the status of the warranty before you purchase it).

Warranties can vary - they offer different protection, from the most basic cover to those which provide comprehensive cover. For instance, you may be covered only for the 'market value' of the goods, which means their second hand value after use or you may be covered 'new for old'. Do not assume that a warranty will provide cover for all problems encountered with the goods. They usually have exclusions that set limits on the cover you receive.

A warranty or extended warranty is additional to the legal rights you have as a consumer and must not affect those rights in any way.

What legal protection do I get with warranties and guarantees?

The Sale and Supply of Goods to Consumers Regulations 2002 states that if a guarantee provider offers a guarantee on goods sold or supplied to consumers, the provider takes on a contractual obligation to honour the conditions set out in the guarantee. For example, if the guarantee provider refuses to repair goods as set out under the terms of the guarantee, you can take legal action against the provider of the guarantee for breach of contract. This could be claiming back the cost of repairs if you have had them carried out elsewhere.

The guarantee should be written in English and the terms should be set out in plain intelligible language. The name and address of the guarantee provider, the duration of the guarantee and the location it covers must also be given. You have the right to ask the provider to make the guarantee available to you in writing or any other durable form available.

If you have a problem with an insurance backed extended warranty that was sold to you, and you have been unable to resolve it with the warranty provider, you are entitled to take your complaint to the Financial Ombudsman Service. For problems with non insurance backed extended warranties, contact the Citizens Advice consumer service.

The Supply of Extended Warranties on Domestic Electrical Goods Order 2005 requires traders that supply extended warranties on domestic electrical goods to provide consumers with certain information before the sale of the extended warranty.

Traders supplying this type of extended warranty are required to:

- clearly display the price and duration of the warranty
- make it clear that the warranty is optional
- give you information on your statutory rights
- inform you that the warranty does not have to be purchased at the time the goods are purchased
- provide details of cancellation and termination rights
- inform you that warranties may be available elsewhere
- provide a statement on the financial protection consumers have if the provider of the extended warranty goes out of business
- state whether or not the warranty will cease if a claim is made
- inform you that your household insurance may be relevant to the purchase of the goods
- give a quotation in writing and inform you that the quotation price is valid for at least 30 days if the warranty costs more than £20
- allow you to cancel it within 45 days and get a refund if a claim has not been made and if the warranty that was supplied has an initial duration of more than one year
- allow you to cancel it and receive a pro rata refund after 45 days even if a claim has been made and if the warranty that was supplied has an initial duration of more than one year

If insurance backed guarantees and warranties are marketed and sold at a distance - without face to face contact between the consumer and trader, such as online - the Financial Services (Distance Marketing) Regulations 2004 apply. These regulations cover the distance marketing of consumer financial services and specify the information that must be given to you before and after a contract is concluded. You have the right to cancel a financial services distance contract and the cancellation period for this type of insurance is 14 calendar days which runs from the day after the day the contract is concluded. Guarantees and warranties are in addition to the statutory rights you have under the Consumer Rights Act 2015.

What should I consider before I buy an extended warranty?

- consider whether you actually need an extended warranty - for example, does your home insurance policy provide all the cover you need?
- there are a wide variety of warranty providers, so shop around for the best warranty at the right price before you buy. You don't have to buy in-store at the same time as buying the accompanying product
- be careful when purchasing extended warranties that are paid for on a monthly basis as long term these can be very expensive
- watch out for high pressure selling of warranties at the point of sale
- ensure you have clear information on the costs and the benefits of the warranty
- it is important to find out what the warranty **does not** cover

Some frequently asked questions

Q. I bought a fridge/freezer 18 months ago and the freezer section has completely failed. I went back to the shop, but they refused to do anything as it was outside the original 12 month guarantee. What are my rights?

A. If the time limit has expired on the guarantee, you cannot make a claim. However, if you can show that the goods were not of satisfactory quality at the time of sale then you may have a claim against the trader under the Consumer Rights Act 2015

Q. I had damp-proofing work carried out on my house five years ago by a limited company but I've noticed some rising damp under a bay window. I didn't think this should have happened so soon. I complained to the company that carried out the work as I had been told it was covered by a ten year guarantee. However, the company claims that the original company went into liquidation and it is an entirely separate legal entity. It is refusing to honour the guarantee or carry out any remedial work unless I pay. Can they do this?

A. Your contract for the work and the guarantee was with the original limited company, and it is liable to you only for as long as it is trading. If it ceases trading or the premises have been taken over by another business, you cannot enforce the guarantee. If you paid for the work using a credit card or on finance arranged by the company, the finance provider may be equally liable (which means equally responsible) with the company under Section 75 of the Consumer Credit Act 1974. In this case, you could claim from the finance provider instead of the company. Some companies offer insurance-backed guarantees for this sort of work. This means that the guarantee is underwritten by an insurance company and exists in its own right, separate from the company that carried out the work. If the company disappears or goes bust, you should still be able to make a claim under the guarantee from the insurance company for the lifetime of the guarantee. Check your guarantee carefully.

Q. I bought a used car six weeks ago and the dealer persuaded me to buy a 12 month warranty. I thought that this would cover me for everything that went wrong during this period. The cambelt has just failed and this has led to a very high repair bill. However, the warranty company have just pointed to a clause in the policy that excludes liability for cambelt failures and the dealer won't pay for the repair. What are my rights?

A. With any warranty it is essential that you read the terms and conditions before you decide to buy it. The warranty company may be entitled to rely on this exclusion clause. You still have a contract with the dealer who sold you the car. You could argue that the dealer is in breach of contract and that under the Consumer Rights Act 2015 the car is not of satisfactory quality.

Q. I had a builder in to build a small extension last year. He told me that all his work was 'guaranteed' but I didn't get anything in writing. The pointing in the brickwork is now defective, but he refuses to put it right. When I mentioned the guarantee, he said: 'What guarantee?' What rights do I have against him?

A. This shows the importance of getting a written guarantee. Without this, it is impossible to prove that you were offered a guarantee, or indeed, what the extent of the cover might be. Remember that you have a contract with the builder under the Consumer Rights Act 2015 and he should have carried out the work with reasonable care and skill.

Q.I bought a new motorbike last year that came with a manufacturer's six year anti-corrosion and paintwork guarantee. The exhaust has started to rust and the paint on the tank is peeling so the bike will probably need major re-painting and re-chroming work, which will be costly. The manufacturer is refusing to honour the guarantee and, as this was one of my main reasons for buying this brand, I am very annoyed. What should I do?

A. Even though you did not pay for it, the guarantee provider takes on a contractual obligation to honour the terms of the guarantee under the Sale and Supply of Goods to Consumers Regulations 2002. You are entitled to take legal action against the manufacturer. You can also complain to the dealer who you bought the motorbike from as you have rights under the Consumer Rights Act 2015 if the motorbike is not of satisfactory quality.

Q. I've heard that under European Union (EU) law I'm allowed a two year minimum guarantee on goods. Is that correct?

A. EU Directive 1999/44/EC states that all European Union member states must allow consumers to make a claim for faulty or misdescribed goods under their consumer rights for a minimum of two years. English law already allows you to make a claim for up to six years from the date you bought the goods and for up to five years in Scotland. Therefore if you buy any goods from any other EU member state, you can assume that you can make a claim for faulty or misdescribed goods for at least two years after.

Q. I bought an extended insurance backed warranty online. I have changed my mind and want to cancel. What can I do?

A. You have the right to cancel within 14 calendar days from the day after the day you bought the warranty. You should check the website for details of how you can exercise your right to cancel and then inform the supplier. The supplier must refund your money within 30 calendar days from the day you cancelled.

Q. I think that the trader deliberately misled me over the guarantee. What can I do?

A. The trader may have breached the Consumer Protection from Unfair Trading Regulations 2008 which prohibits traders from engaging in unfair trading practices. You should contact the Citizens Advice consumer service, which will be able to advise you, as well as referring your case to trading standards for further investigation.

****

Chapter 6

Denying Liability For Products

In the last chapter, we looked at guarantees and warranties and the rights and obligations of the consumer. In this chapter we will look at attempts to exclude or deny liability for a product.

We have all seen notices on products which say that the manufacturer is excluded from all liability for a good. This is a very important area and we need to look at the actual liability of a manufacturer even if an exclusion notice has been given. There is nothing stopping a shopkeeper or manufacturer from stonewalling your claim for damages due to the fact that an exclusion notice has been attached to a product.

Typical exclusion notices might read:

"No responsibility will be accepted for goods once they have left the store"
"There will be no refund for this good, even if found to be unsuitable"
"We accept no returns under any circumstances"

The list is endless and can apply to a whole range of products. However, what the consumer needs to know is whether a retailer can actually impose any of these restrictions. Can a retailer avoid the liabilities imposed under the current legislation, the Consumer Rights Act 2015?

There is one major starting point for all exclusion notices. What we need to determine is whether or not the notice has been incorporated, or is an integral part of, the contract for sale. If this has not occurred then there can be no exclusion notice. Incorporation means that if a consumer signs a contract they are bound by it, in the absence of any sort of misrepresentation. So, if a consumer has signed a contract they are bound by its terms. However, if the terms contained in an unsigned document which is an exclusion notice, the terms will only form part of the actual contract if there has been an attempt to bring the notice to the consumers attention.

The Consumer Rights Act 2015 is of importance in determining whether or not a consumer has signed an unfair, or onerous contract. The Act will govern any clause which purports or attempts to restrict liability. The Act governs business and will control the acts of a person who, through contract, attempts to deny any liability for a good where, in fact, there does exist a liability in law.

If we look at the matter objectively, as we have seen so far there are a range of laws which protect the consumer and place obligations on manufacturers and suppliers. Merely to insert an exclusion clause, thereby giving full protection against the law, is an absurdity.

Example A removal firm undertakes to do a job for Mr and Mrs Smith. They inform the couple that their liability for any damages to goods is covered by an exclusion clause in a contract that they wish to sign. This states that liability for any damage is limited to £35 per item or £100 in total.

Can they do this? What they are trying to do is to avoid the above Act which impose liabilities for negligence and the answer would be no, they cannot limit there own liability.

A very important point to note is that if you are dealing with a retailer as a consumer then the retailer cannot avoid responsibility as contained in the implied terms of contract which are governed by the Consumer Rights Act 2015.

There may be occasions where other goods, such as exchanged goods, hire goods or the materials part of a contract are concerned and the CRA 2015 will apply.

The Unfair Contract Terms Act 1977 also covered negligence based clauses, i.e., where a manufacturer denies liability for negligence. Section 1 of the UCTA defines negligence as the breach of duty of care arising in contract. The 2015 CRA will now apply.

As far as the consumer is concerned, the area which is most likely to arise is an attempt to avoid liability for a breach of the CRA 2015.

Section 2 of the Unfair Contract Terms Act stated that any clause (or notice) was invalid insofar as it attempts to exclude liability for negligence *resulting in death or personal injury. This is now replaced by the CRA 2015.*

The Act states that if any other loss or damage arises as a result then the clause of the notice will only be valid provided a reasonableness test is satisfied. The reasonableness test contains guidelines and include:

a) the strength of the bargaining position between parties to a contract
b) whether there was any inducement to agree to the term, i.e., was there any special offer or was the consumer put in a position where he/ she had to agree before purchase;
c) whether the consumer knew of any term in the first place;
d) whether the goods were specially manufactured.

The Unfair Contract Terms Act also dealt with other breaches of contract such as where a business will try to exclude or restrict liability to a certain sum or claims to be entitled to give a good or service which is in fact substantially different to that stated. A common example here is that of a tour operator stating that they have the right to offer alternative holidays. The UCTA also covered the notice which claims to have no liability for the non delivery of a service.

Section 4 of the Act stated that a person dealing as a consumer cannot be made to indemnify another person against liability for negligence or breach of contract unless the reasonableness test has been passed. Section 5 dealt with manufacturers guarantees to the consumer and states that if goods which are supplied for private use or consumption prove defective whilst in use and cause loss or damage as a result of negligence in manufacture or distribution, then any attempt to avoid liability in a guarantee is void. If misrepresentation is involved, then any attempt to exclude liability for misrepresentation is only valid provided that the reasonableness test is passed.

As stated the Unfair Terms in Consumer Contracts Act has now been replaced by the Consumer Rights Act 2015.

There are areas of law which will make it a criminal liability to give an exclusion notice. The Consumer Rights Act 2015 , makes it a criminal offence to use a void exemption clause in a contract. Therefore, a notice such as no refunds etc, can make the seller criminally liable. The order also makes it an offence to supply goods to a consumer with written exclusion notices without pointing out that a consumers statutory rights are unaffected.

The effect of the European Community and European Directives.
There are attempts to make liability for consumer goods standard throughout the European Community and there is a European Directive on unfair terms in Consumer contracts which will seek to give the consumer more power, particularly when dealing with large companies or corporations. Contracts which operate to the detriment of the consumer will not be allowed. The draft directive is concerned only with contracts between business and consumers. No contracts will be excluded from the directive.

****

Chapter 7

Unsolicited Goods

Unsolicited goods are those which are sent to a person without their requesting them. This has caused problems for consumers where delivery was inevitably followed by aggressive sales tactics, such as sending an invoice for a price. This problem was originally overcome by the Unsolicited Goods and Services Act 1971 which gave protection in both civil law and criminal law.

The area of unsolicited goods (previously covered by the Unsolicited Goods and Services Act 1971 and the Consumer Protection (Distance Selling) Regulations 2000) is now covered by the Consumer Contracts (Information, Cancellation and Additional Charges) Regulations 2013. These regulations came into force in June 2014.

The regulations state that where:

- unsolicited goods are sent to a person with a view to his acquiring them; and
- the recipient has no reasonable cause to believe that they were sent with a view to their being acquired for the purpose of business and the recipient has not agreed to acquire the goods or to return them.

Where these conditions are fulfilled, the recipient and the sender, the recipient may use, deal with or dispose of the goods as if they were an absolute gift.

The regulations also provide that the rights of the sender to the goods are extinguished.

Criminal law

If you receive a demand for payment for unsolicited goods or services, you can ignore it. If the trader does this, they may have committed a criminal offence under the Consumer Protection from Unfair Trading Regulations 2008 (see Chapter 11). You should report the matter to your trading standards department through Citizens Advice.

It is also an offence to:

- assert a right to payment; or
- threaten to bring legal proceedings in respect of the goods; or
- place or threaten to place the name of any person on a defaulter list; or
- invoke or threaten to invoke any other collection procedure.

****

Chapter 8

Consumer Contracts (Information, Cancellation and Additional Charges) Regulations 2013 - Including Digital Content and Distance Selling

In the previous chapter, we looked at consumer rights when a manufacturer attempts to deny or to exclude liability. In this chapter we will look at new legislation, which came into force on 14th June 2014, The Consumer Contracts (Information, Cancellation and Additional Charges) Regulations 2013 which covers, or rather strengthens, the rights of consumers, and compliments existing legislation so far covered in this book, when purchasing goods, either on business premises, off the premises (such as workplace or home) or from a distance, i.e. over the internet. The Regulations also cover digital content, such as software.

The 2013 Regulations replace the Consumer Protection (Distance Selling) Regulations 2000 (for contracts made after June 2014) and the Cancellation of Contracts Made in a Consumer's Home or Place of Work Regulations 2008 (albeit these latter provisions still apply to contracts made before 13 June 2014).

The 2013 Regulations run alongside another piece of legislation covered in chapter 8, the Consumer Rights (Payment Surcharges) Regulations 2012 which came into force 6th April 2013. these regulations are phased and will apply to all businesses from 14th June 2014.

The 2013 Regulations and buying 'On premises'

Traders must comply with the Regulations when they sell goods, services and digital content to consumers from their business premises. They have to give you certain information before they make a contract with you and get your clear agreement if they want to charge for 'extras'. telephone helplines must only be charged at a basic rate and there are clear rules on delivery and the point at which the consumer becomes responsible for the goods.

Contracts the regulations apply to

The Regulations apply to:

- Sales contracts-contracts for the sale of goods and contracts for the supply of goods and services such as mobile phones with airtime.
- Service contracts, which are contracts for the supply of services only
- Contracts for digital content, such as contracts for data which is produced and supplied in a digital form, such as music and film downloads.

Contracts the Regulations don't cover

Some contracts, which are covered by other regulations are excluded from the 2013 Regulations. They are:

Gambling, including lotteries Services of a banking, credit, insurance, personal pension, investment or payment nature

- Construction and the sale of immovable property
- Rental of residential accommodation
- Construction of new buildings or virtually new buildings by the conversion of existing buildings
- Supply of food and drink and other consumables by traders on regular rounds to home, residence or workplace
- Package travel, holidays and toursTimeshare, long term holiday products, resale and exchange contracts
- Goods sold from automatic vending machines
- Contracts made from a public phone and via one single connection by phone, internet or fax
- Goods sold by authority of law

Provision of information

The Regulations place a responsibility on the trader, whilst you are in a store, which includes a market place, to provide you with clear and understandable information before you enter into a contract. the information should cover the following:

- The main characteristics of the goods, service or digital content that you are about to purchase
- Full details of the trader, identity, address and telephone number

- Total price of the goods and services including all taxes. If the price cannot be worked out in advance, you must be given the method of calculation
- Additional delivery charges
- Payment, delivery and performance arrangements
- Any existing complaints policy
- Details of any after sales service and guarantee
- Length of the contract (where applicable) or if the contract does not have a set length details of how the contract can be ended
- Digital content functionality such as regional coding and any other technical protection measures where applicable
- Digital content compatibility with relevant hardware and software.

The above information forms part of the contract that you have with the trader and if the fail to provide information or it is incorrect then you can sue for breach of contract.

Additional payments under the contract

If you are offered extras, such as gift wrapping or special delivery that is linked to the main contract, the trader must get your agreement to charge you for it. The trader cannot simply have a tick box on the order form for example, that you have to un-tick or ask the trader to remove. If extra charges have not been agreed then you don't have to pay for them.

Telephone helpline charges

If a trader provides a telephone helpline for you to contact them about the goods or services you have purchased, they can only charge you the basic rate. This is to stop profiteering from the use of such lines. Basic rate means the normal geographic or mobile rate.

Delivery

The trader is under an obligation to deliver goods to you unless you have agreed otherwise. The goods must be delivered no later than 30 days after the day on which you entered into the contract. You can, if you so wish, agree your own delivery terms with the trader.

If there are problems with the delivery, such as the trader refusing to deliver the goods then you are entitled to cancel the contract. If you have ordered multiple goods and some of them are not delivered on time then you can cancel the goods that have not been delivered.

Responsibility for goods

You become responsible for the goods when you, or a person authorised by you, takes actual possession of them. If you organise your own carrier then the trader is only responsible until the carrier takes possession of them.

Buying at home-Off-Premises contracts

Traders must comply with the Regulations when they sell goods, services and digital content to consumers away from their business premises, such as on your doorstep, in your home or place of work. these are called 'off premises' contracts.

You have the right to cancel most off premises contracts and the cancellation period is 14 days. Traders must give certain information before they enter into a contract with you and musty get your clear agreement before they charge for extras. Telephone helplines must be charged at the basic rate and there are clear rules on delivery. If the trader sends you unsolicited goods you can keep them and do not have to pay for them. Any other right as outlined throughout this book are not affected in an way.

Definition of an off premises contract

An off premises contract is:

- When you buy goods, services or digital content away from a trader's business premises but with the trader present, such as in your home or workplace
- If a trader organises a trip to promote their goods or services
- If you make an offer to buy with the trader present, but that offer is not made on the traders business premises
- If a contract is concluded on business premises or by distance after trader has communicated to you when they were not on their business premises.
- The regulations apply to sales contracts, service contracts and digital content-contracts for data which is produced and supplied in digital form.
- There are excluded contracts as below:
- Gambling, including lotteries

- Services of a banking, credit, insurance, personal pension, investment or payment nature
- Construction and the sale of immovable property
- Rental of residential accommodation
- Construction of new buildings or virtually new buildings by the conversion of existing buildings
- Supply of food and drink and other consumables by traders on regular rounds to home, residence or workplace
- Package travel, holidays and tours
- Timeshare, long term holiday products, resale and exchange contracts
- Goods sold from automatic vending machines
- Contracts made from a public phone and via one single connection by phone, internet or fax
- Goods sold by authority of law

Provision of information

The trader must give you information in the same was as for on premises contracts. However, there is a slight difference. If you ask the trader to perform a repair or maintenance service immediately and it is less than £170, the trader does not have to provide the information required by the Regulations.

Notwithstanding this, there are still rules that they must satisfy before the contract is made-they must supply their name and trading address, price and delivery cost and details about their products and services plus any cancellation rights and an explanation of the circumstances when there are no cancellation rights. After the contract is made the trader must give you a copy of the signed contract or confirmation of the contract in a durable form, such as paper or email.

Contracts that cannot be cancelled
- NHS medicinal products or services
- Passenger transport services
- Contracts for not more than £42
- Supply of goods or services (not utilities)
- Supply of goods that have been made to your specification or clearly personalised
- Supply of goods that can deteriorate rapidly such as flowers
- Supply of alcohol where the contract price is fixed, delivery is after 30 days and the value depends on fluctuations in the market
- Contracts where you request a visit from a contractor to carry out emergency repairs or maintenance
- Supply of newspapers, periodicals or magazines
- Contracts made at a public auction. Internet auctions are not public auctions so must give you cancellation rights
- Supply of accommodation, transport of goods, vehicle rental, catering or services relating to leisure activities if the contract states when the service has to be performed.

Rights to cancel contracts
The regulations give you the right to cancel a contract at any time for any reason within the cancellation period. You also have the

right to withdraw your offer to buy before a contract is made. This is 14 days in most cases. If the trader does not provide you with information on your cancellation rights, the cancellation period can be extended by up to 12 months, depending on when or if the information is provided. It is a criminal offence if the trader fails to give you a notice of your rights to cancel.

Other responsibilities
All other responsibilities as outlined above for on premises contracts apply.

Distance selling (buying by internet, phone and mail order)
As mentioned, the Consumer Protection (Distance Selling Regulations) 2000 have been replaced in their entirety for goods purchased after June 2014.

Cancellation
You have the right to cancel most distance contracts within 14 days. Other conditions the same as on or off premises trading apply such as the obligation to provide information before entering into a contract with you

Contracts to which the regulations apply
• Sales contracts-contracts for the sale of goods and contracts for the supply of goods and services such as mobile phones with airtime. Also, service contracts, which are contracts for the supply of services only

- Contracts for digital content, such as contracts for data which is produced and supplied in a digital form, such as music and film downloads.

Not all sales, service and digital contracts are covered by the regulations but there are rights under other legislation, as outlined in this book.

Excluded contracts are:

- Gambling, including lotteries
- Services of a banking, credit, insurance, personal pension, investment or payment nature
- Construction and the sale of immovable property
- Rental of residential accommodation
- Construction of new buildings or virtually new buildings by the conversion of existing buildings
- Supply of food and drink and other consumables by traders on regular rounds to home, residence or workplace
- Package travel, holidays and tours
- Timeshare, long term holiday products, resale and exchange contracts
- Goods sold from automatic vending machines
- Contracts made from a public phone and via one single connection by phone, internet or fax
- Goods sold by authority of law

Information

When you buy goods, services or digital content under a distance contract you are entitled to the following information, much the same as on or off premises contracts:

- The main characteristics of the goods, service or digital content that you are about to purchase
- Full details of the trader, identity, address and telephone number
- Total price of the goods and services including all taxes. If the price cannot be worked out in advance, you must be given the method of calculation
- Additional delivery charges
- Payment, delivery and performance arrangements
- Any existing complaints policy
- Details of any after sales service and guarantee
- Length of the contract (where applicable) or if the contract does not have a set length details of how the contract can be ended
- Digital content functionality such as regional coding and any other technical protection measures where applicable
- Digital content compatibility with relevant hardware and software.

As with other areas covered under the regulations, if the trader does not supply you with this information then you do not have to pay these charges. As with on or off premises contracts there are certain contracts you cant cancel, as listed above. The Consumer Contracts (Information, Cancellation and Additional Charges)

Regulations 2013 are additional protective measures and reinforce existing legislation.

****

Chapter 9

Consumer Rights (Payment Surcharges) Regulations 2012 as Amended

---

Consumer Rights (Payment Surcharges) Regulations 2012 as amended by the Payment Services Regulations 2017
If a business permits customers to make payment for goods and services by a credit card or a debit card, and a charge is made for offering this payment facility, then the Consumer Rights (Payment Surcharges) Regulations 2012, as amended by the Payment Services Regulations 2017 apply. The Regulations aim to clarify consumer rights in relation to the payment methods used when buying goods and services.

The purpose of the Regulations is to:

- increase price transparency, which will enable consumers to choose effectively between different products and services
- make the charges reflective of the actual cost to business
- encourage fair competition

New rules prohibit traders from levelling a surcharge in relation to a wide variety of transactions, and surcharges are limited in some other circumstances. This prohibition came into force on 13 January 2018.

Restrictions on payment charges

The Consumer Rights (Payment Surcharges) Regulations 2012 came into force on 6 April 2013 and apply to contracts entered into on or after that date. The Regulations will still allow a business to make a charge for credit or debit card payments. However, if the customer has to pay a surcharge for using the credit or debit card then that surcharge must not be higher than the cost the business has to pay for processing that method of payment. The Regulations do not specify any maximum amounts as the costs should reflect the actual cost to the individual business of processing the payment.

Methods of payment extend beyond debit and credit cards and include (but are not limited to) cash, cheques, prepaid cards, charge cards, credit transfers and direct debits. As the technology relating to payments develops, any new methods of paying will also be subject to the Regulations.

A business can apply the payment surcharge on the basis of the average cost incurred in processing payment by a particular means.

Businesses may still also charge booking fees and administrative fees as long as these fees remain constant irrespective of the method of payment. For example, the booking fee will be £10 whether payment for the booking is paid by cash or by a debit card.

Definitions of businesses and consumers

The Regulations only apply to contracts concluded between businesses and consumers. A consumer is a person who enters the contract for purposes that are wholly or mainly outside the person's trade, business, craft or profession.

A business is a person acting for purposes relating to that person's trade, business, craft or profession whether they are an individual, partnership or an organisation.

Business-to-business contracts are **not** subject to the Regulations.

Application of the Regulations

The Regulations apply to contracts however they are concluded. They will therefore apply regardless of the method of sale. They cover contracts concluded on business premises, contracts concluded away from business premises, and those concluded at a distance (for example, a purchase via the internet or on the telephone).

Excluded business sectors

Some specific business sectors have been excluded from the Regulations. The Regulations were introduced on a phased basis, dependent on the size of the business, but are applicable to all types of businesses from 12 June 2014 (other than those categorised as exempt).

Excluded contracts

The Regulations do **not** apply to certain excluded contracts, which are listed below:

- contracts for social services including social housing, childcare and support of families and persons permanently or temporarily in need, including long-term care

- contracts for health services provided, whether or not via healthcare facilities, by health professionals to patients to assess, maintain or restore their state of health, including the prescription, dispensation and provision of medicinal products and medical devices
- contracts for gambling within the meaning of the Gambling Act 2005
- contracts for services of a banking, credit, insurance, personal pension, investment or payment nature
- contracts for the creation of immovable property or of rights in immovable property
- contracts for rental of accommodation for residential purposes
- contracts for the construction of new buildings, or the construction of substantially new buildings by the conversion of existing buildings
- contracts that fall within the scope of European law relating to the protection of consumers in respect of certain aspects of timeshare, long-term holiday products, resale and exchange contracts
- contracts for the supply of foodstuffs, beverages or other goods intended for current consumption in the household that are supplied by a trader on frequent and regular rounds to the consumer's home, residence or workplace
- contracts concluded by means of automatic vending machines or automated commercial premises
- contracts concluded with a telecommunications operator through a public telephone for the use of the telephone

- contracts concluded for the use of one single connection, by telephone, internet or fax, established by a consumer
- contracts by way of execution or otherwise by authority of law

Enforcement

The Consumer Protection from Unfair Trading Regulations 2008 are important in respect of the transparency and presentation of payment surcharges. Whilst the CPRs have no effect on the cost of any payment surcharge, they do prohibit any unfair commercial practices that may affect a consumer's transactional decision making. This could include 'misleading actions' and/or 'misleading omissions'.

If an enforcement body can establish a breach of the payment surcharges provision and demonstrate collective harm they can ask the court can grant an enforcement order. This can require that the trader does not continue or repeat the conduct. These orders are intended to prevent the usage of the unreasonable payment charges and to prohibit future breaches of the Regulations to protect consumers.

Consumers' right of redress

The Regulations also provide for consumers to be able to seek redress themselves irrespective of any public enforcement if the contract subjects them to an unreasonable payment surcharge. Regulation 10 states that where a business charges a fee in contravention of the prohibition against excess payment surcharges, payment of the fee is unenforceable or, if it has already been paid, the fee is refundable. The consumer may take legal action to enforce these rights and recover their money.

The Payment Services Regulations 2017

The Payment Service Regulations 2017 (the 'Regulations') replaced the Payment Services Regulations 2009 and set out the rules relating to all 'payment services' including the services provided by banks, building societies and debit card providers.

It brings the European payments law, known as the second Payment Services Directive - or PSD2 - into UK law.

The Regulations also outline what consumers can expect their bank to do if there has been unauthorised use of their account details or their debit cards. The principles in the Regulations sets out the rules that all service providers (including banks, building societies and card providers) must follow.

Payment Service Regulations 2017, what to claim?

The Payment Service Regulations 2017 set out what payment service providers must do if there has been unauthorised or fraudulent activity on an account. Subject to the exceptions noted, a person should be able to get your money back as long as the provider can't prove that a person hadn't taken reasonable steps to keep their card or account information secure.

Lost or stolen debit card

If a persons debit card is lost or stolen and then used to buy something, and that person reports the unauthorised transactions without undue delay, their debit card provider should refund them immediately.

However this is subject to the following exceptions:

- If the debit card provider can show that a person failed to take reasonable steps to protect your their features (e.g. your PIN), then it can make a £50 deduction from any refund it pays to that person
- If a debit card provider can show that a person acted fraudulently, it can refuse to give a refund
- If it can show a person was grossly negligent in not taking reasonable care of their card's security features (e.g. their PIN), the card provider would have grounds to refuse to refund any of the sum disputed - except where the card or card details were used to make a distance contract under the Consumer Contracts Regulations (e.g. online or on the phone)

However, the debit card provider can't make any deduction or refuse to refund a person if the disputed transaction was made after a person had reported the card lost or stolen. If the unauthorised payment(s) caused a person to incur interest or any other charges (such as an overdraft fee, for example), the debit card provider must also refund those charges so that a person is in the position they would have been in if the unauthorised payment had not taken place.

Credit cards

These provisions don't apply to credit cards as the Consumer Credit Act 1974 already sets out rules that apply to credit cards. The Consumer Credit Act says that if a persons credit card is lost or stolen and used without their consent, the most a person should be responsible for is the first £50 of any unauthorised transactions made before they reported the card missing.

Unauthorised debit transactions

The Regulations can also help if there is a transaction from a persons debit account that they didn't authorise. For example, if their debit card has not been lost or stolen and someone else uses the card details to buy something (for example if a card is cloned, the account data is lost in a data breach, or someone uses details given to a retailer when buying an item over the phone or online), then the Regulations mean a person should be refunded in full as long as your report the unauthorised transaction promptly.

The Regulations treat unauthorised card usage the same as they do lost or stolen cards. As outlined above, if a provider can show that a person hadn't taken reasonable steps to protect the security of a card (i.e. the PIN or online security details) a person could be liable for the first £35 of any loss they incur. And if a persons provider can show that the cardholder acted fraudulently, they won't be entitled to any refund. As with lost or stolen cards, if a person was grossly negligent, then the service provider can refuse to credit any money back to them - except where their card or account details were used to enter into a distance contract under the Consumer Contract Regulations.

Card payment surcharges banned

Retailers and traders are no longer allowed to charge a surcharge for using a credit or debit card when making a purchase.

Increased security

The regulations require stronger customer authentication to reduce the risk of fraud. This means that in order to access data or accounts, a person will have to take two or more independent actions in order to log in. This could include:

- Knowledge – something only a person knows (password, PIN, etc.)
- Possession – something only a person possesses (card or other material)
- Inherence – something such as fingerprint, voice or facial recognition)

For remote transactions - internet, mobile - a unique authentication code will dynamically link transactions to the respective amount and payee

****

Chapter 10

Consumers and Credit

In the previous chapter we looked at the introduction of the Consumer Contracts (Information, Cancellation and Additional Charges) Regulations 2013, which cover sales on and off premises and also distance selling. They also cover digital content. In this chapter we will look at the all-important area of consumer credit.

Consumer credit in the UK is regulated by the Consumer Credit Act 1974 (amended in 2006), the Financial Services and Markets Act 2000 and various regulations implementing European Union consumer credit law.

The most important of the Acts dealing with consumers and credit is the Consumer Credit Act 1974. This act also encompasses loans from pawnbrokers and also payday loans. This has been supplemented by the Consumer Credit (Advertising) Regulations 2011 (see further on in this chapter).

Nowadays, many people use credit to help them with their buying. It helps to spread the load, especially with expensive items such as furniture or cars. But borrowing can be costly and with so many different types of credit available, it is wise to shop around before you sign any credit agreement.

Using a credit card when buying a single item costing over £100 but under £30,000 can provide extra protection if you have a problem with your purchase. Whether you use your credit card to pay the full amount or even part of the deposit (as little as £1 but no more than £25,000), the credit card company is legally bound to help in cases of faulty goods or non-delivery if the retailer goes out of business.

Be warned, however, that you may not be protected if your payment is made through a third party - see the section below on credit cards. The main law to give you protection when buying on credit is the Consumer Credit Act 1974. By law you're entitled to a copy of your credit agreement so make sure you get one. Never sign a blank form or even leave some sections blank.

Right of withdrawal

You have a right to withdraw from a credit agreement without giving any reason, within 14 days. When the 14 day period begins will depend on when the agreement is made and there must be information in the agreement telling you about your withdrawal rights. On withdrawal you must repay the amount of money received and any interest accrued.

Credit cards

Under section 75 of the Consumer Credit Act 1974, if you use your credit card to buy a single item costing more than £100 but no more than £30,000, you can claim from the credit card company or the trader if something goes wrong. Many websites use an online payment processor such as Paypal, Worldpay or Google Checkout.

While the law in this area is not certain, you may not be covered by the protection offered by section 75. Online payment processors do have their own refund systems, so make sure you read their terms and conditions carefully. If you use a credit card to buy airline or other travel tickets from a travel agent you cannot normally claim against the travel agent if the airline delays or cancels the flight as they were contracted to supply the ticket, not the flight. However, if you use a credit card to buy the travel agent's own package of travel arrangements the agent then becomes the supplier of the holiday package and has equal liability with the credit card company.

Credit card fees banned

As we discussed in the previous chapter, the surcharges added to credit card transactions—which can range from as little as 50p and sometimes as high as 20 percent of a total transaction—are banned from 13th January 2018. Low cost airlines, food delivery apps, and ticketing services are some of the worst offenders, although several government agencies and local councils also charge for the use of a credit card. Debit cards are typically exempt, but smaller convenience stores are known to apply a surcharge, regardless of card type.

The ban builds on an EU directive launched in 2015, which capped the "interchange fee" paid by the merchant at no more than 0.3 percent for credit cards and 0.2 percent for debit cards. At the time, the EU noted that the surcharges, which are only supposed to reflect the cost of processing payments, generated as much €13 billion a year across Europe.

Airlines were routinely criticised by consumers for the credit card charges they applied to ticket purchases. Ryanair and EasyJet applied a credit card fee of two percent and one percent respectively. While, many online travel agents and flight resellers also charged a fee of around two percent, regardless of the airline being booked. Ticketmaster didn't list a specific credit card fee, but did apply a "service charge" on top of an "order processing fee" and occasionally a "facility fee." Empire cinemas charged a 70p "card handling fee," while food delivery app HungryHouse charged 50p per credit card transaction.

A significant number of local authorities and government agencies also charged a fee. HM Revenue & Customs charges between 0.374 percent and 2.406 percent, depending on whether a personal or corporate card was used to pay taxes, while the Driver and Vehicle Licensing Agency (DVLA) currently added a flat fee of £2.50 to vehicle tax payments by credit card.

While the UK ban falls in line with the EU directive, the government claimed it will go further by banning charges for American Express cards and users of services such as Apple Pay and PayPal, which typically apply a higher fee than the likes of Visa and Mastercard. As the EU noted last year, usually, competition leads to lower prices since companies compete by offering lower prices than their competitors.

In the case of interchange fees, the opposite occurs. Since issuing banks benefit from interchange fee revenues [by directly receiving the payment], card schemes compete for the issuing banks by offering higher interchange fees.

These fees are a cost for retailers which increase the price of their products. Interchange fees are therefore, indirectly, paid by consumers. Consumers and retailers are often unaware of the level of these fees. In addition, cardholders are encouraged through rewards offered by their bank to use cards that generate higher fees for the bank. However, small traders—for whom the cost of processing a card payment can be significant—will no longer be able to list their card fees outright. Some worry this may lead to small traders refusing to accept card payments altogether, although it's more likely that—like large retailers—they will either absorb the fee or raise prices to compensate for the loss.

Credit reference agencies

You don't have a right to credit. Before giving you credit, lenders want to check whether you're an acceptable risk. To help them do this they may check with firms called Credit Reference Agencies (CRAs).

These agencies don't keep 'black lists' or give an opinion as to whether or not you should be given credit. They just provide information about your credit record. You are entitled to see a copy of any information they hold on you and to correct anything in it that you can prove is wrong.

You are entitled to see a copy of your file if you make a written request and send £2. Online and telephone requests may cost more. The contact details of the credit reference agencies are shown below and you can also find more information on the website of the Money Advice Service. The CRA commits a criminal offence if it fails to correct files.

Credit unions

To borrow from a credit union you must first become a member and show by saving regularly over a set period that you will be able to afford the repayments. This is an excellent way of getting credit as the interest rate is usually lower than that used by other lenders.

Hire purchase

You cannot end a hire purchase agreement unless you are up to date with your payments. You will have to pay at least half of the total hire purchase price. You cannot sell the goods until the agreement has been paid off.

Logbook loans

Consumers will regularly see these loans being advertised on the high street or on the internet promising cash fast, but they can often prove to be more problematic than beneficial for borrowers. A logbook loan is a loan secured on your vehicle. You will be asked to hand over the logbook (V5 form - vehicle registration document) and sign a document called a bill of sale. This means that the protection provided by the Consumer Credit Act – that cars cannot be seized without a court order – is removed and the lender can then seize the car if the loan is not paid.

The bill of sale also transfers temporary ownership of your vehicle to the lender, but you are still able to use it while you are making the loan repayments. You only become the legal owner of the vehicle once again when you have settled the agreement in full.

Consumers should consider other types of borrowing before agreeing to a logbook loan, especially if you cannot do without your vehicle. Although these loans provide quick access to money, the APR is likely to be very high, commonly over 200% APR. There may be cheaper ways you can borrow, which do not put you at such a risk of losing your assets. The concept of a logbook loan can be complicated, so if you plan to take one out make sure you ask the lender to explain anything you do not understand. It is vitally important you understand your responsibilities under the agreement to help you minimise the risk of losing your vehicle.

Furthermore, the law only recognises the bill of sale if the lender registers it with the High Court. If it is not registered, the lender must get a court's approval to repossess your vehicle. So if you think you may fall behind with your loan repayments and want to know what will happen to your vehicle, you will need to check if the bill of sale is registered. You will need to give both your and your lender's name and address along with a small fee to the High Court.

Buy now pay later payment options-What is 'buy now, pay later' credit?

Buy now, pay later credit (BNPL) is one of the oldest forms of credit available to people in the UK, going back several decades to before the Financial Services Act came in to force in 1988. BNPL emerged through catalogues and with high-street retailers who realised they could split the payments of expensive items into instalments. Then, as an incentive, they could lure wary shoppers by offering an interest-free period. If you paid off the deal during this timeframe you just paid the price tag. If you went over, however, you could pay 40% interest plus on the original cost of the item.

These deals were controversial. They work on the basis that we shoppers think we'll pay off the item early. In practice, most people fail to do so – and pay a higher price. However, with the rise of online retailers and the emergence of new retail models, this form of credit has been 'reimagined' and repackaged.

It's now often sold more of a lifestyle choice rather than a high interest contract with penalties for defaulting. Much of the blame for this lies with the retailers if they fail to make it clear how the credit works, how much it costs and what happens if you don't pay up on time.

How does it work?
There are two 'main' types of BNPL credit:

The 'old' style – The old model is still widely available online and on the high street. You usually have around 1-2 years interest-free before interest kicks in. Interest rates can no longer be backdated but the costs are still high. The old style of BNPL is usually provided by retailers who are regulated to sell credit or contract out the credit services under their own brand.

The 'new' style – The new model is complicated because it works in regulated (charges interest) and unregulated (doesn't charge interest) forms. Either way, you usually enter into an agreement to either pay in instalments (usually three payments) or longer under a regulated credit deal. Interest rates lower (currently under 20%) but it's harder to keep on top of if you're a regular shopper. Most people now encounter the new form of credit when shopping online. Retailers have 'standard' ways to pay (at the till - online or high street), longer 'old' credit and newer deals all at the same time. The problem is it's immensely hard to keep on top of the number of deals you've got going at any one time – and there's a different set of rules for each way to pay.

Just to give you an idea of how popular BNPL credit is, Resolver www.resolvergroup.com, a complaints handling business free to use, has received 15,814 complaints in less than two years!

How do Klarna and Clearpay fit in to this?

A 'new' form of BNPL credit is becoming ever more popular, with firms like Klarna and Clearpay both offering methods of payment/borrowing when it comes to purchases made (mostly) online. While there's no problem with offering people different ways to pay for goods, the problem with these new businesses is some of their services are unregulated – and though they may not charge you interest or register a black mark on your credit file, our users tell us they've been passed to debt collectors after getting in to difficulties.

Here's how they work.

Klarna

Pay in three instalments – this is interest-free if you meet the payment dates.

Financing – spread over a number of payments (usually up to 36 months) and set by the retailer. Charges and interest apply if defaults occur.

Pay in 30 days – this is the controversial bit. Pay in 30 days works on the basis that you might try before you buy then return (as many retailers sell this form of credit). But at the 30 day point you've bought the goods if you've not returned them.

This payment date range can actually vary from 14 to 30 days depending on the retailer.

Clearpay
Clearpay is a new entrant into this market. It has just one way to pay. Four instalments – payment amount split in to four, fortnightly instalments which are interest-free if paid on time.

What's the problem?
In just a short time, millions of people have signed up to these new payment deals. But they're hard to understand and keep on top of – and all have consequences if you don't pay on time.

There are concerns that this form of credit is unregulated in part and is sold as a 'lifestyle' choice.

The way these deals are set up mean that the retailers are the ones who are supposed to explain how they work/ include warnings on their sites – yet these are often deeply inadequate. It's also really hard to find out what happens if you fail to pay, even on the websites of the credit companies.

Payday loans

Consumers unable to access credit through traditional banking means usually turn to alternative sources, including payday loan companies. Payday, or paycheque loans, are short-term loans that you get in return for your pay cheque or proof of your income. They are basically cash advances on the salary you are expecting and are available online and on the high street. However, there has been a crackdown on payday lenders and the number of lenders has already fallen but there are signs in 2021 that these lenders are on the rise again as a direct result of the Pandemic.

New breed of pay-day loan firms cash in on pandemic

Pay-day loan companies and doorstep lenders are saddling low-income families who have lost jobs because of the coronavirus with loans at interest rates of up to 1,700 per cent. An investigation has discovered a new wave of companies has filled the gap left by businesses such as Wonga after it went bust. Borrowers who take out loans for £1,500 are having to pay back as much as £3,000 after interest. Charities have warned that thousands of people will suffer as a holiday on repayments to help people during the pandemic ends this month.

Provident the UK's biggest doorstep lender, is continuing to visit people at home to collect money in spite of a surge in coronavirus infections. The company has been targeting previous borrowers by offering them cash. One customer said they were enticed into taking a loan after a representative made an unsolicited call with an envelope containing £100 in cash. Another time it is claimed that a collection agent put a foot in the door.

The highest interest rate uncovered is being offered by Little Loans, which offers deals with interest rates of as much as 1,698 per cent. The company claims it brokers loans for 2,451 people every day (about 900,000 loans a year). Last year the company that owns it, Digitonomy, in Cheshire, increased turnover to £312 million, resulting in profits of £4.1 million. It paid directors £1.6 million in dividends. In 2017 it was fined £120,000 for sending millions of unsolicited text messages encouraging people to apply for loans via affiliates.

Customers of Loan Pig will have to pay back £3,000 over the course of six months for loans of £1,500. Step Change, the debt charity, estimates that 980,000 people used at least one form of high-cost credit between the beginning of the coronavirus out-break and early May.

Payday loans can be a way of getting your hands on your wages quicker than you otherwise would, but it is important to be aware of the high interest rates charged and the consequences of falling behind with your repayment. This type of borrowing is not suitable for those looking to repay their loans over a long period, as they are designed to be short-term loans to deal with short-term personal cash flow issues. If loans are rolled over, debts could escalate and consumers could get into difficulties. They should only be considered if consumers are confident that they'll be able to repay the debt in full when it is due.

In October 2018 The City regulator ordered payday lenders to bring forward compensation for customers who were miss-sold loans, even if it threatens the company with bankruptcy.

In strongly worded letters to firms in the high-cost short-term credit market, Jonathan Davidson, the director of supervision at the Financial Conduct Authority (FCA), set out how firms should respond to a recent surge in complaints over unaffordable lending.

It follows the collapse in August of Wonga, the payday lender that became notorious for its extortionate interest rates and was a symbol of Britain's household debt crisis. Wonga was laid low by new rules cutting the amount of interest it could charge, and was finally pushed into administration by a welter of compensation claims for past miss-selling.

If you are considering using a payday loan company, you should look into all the available alternatives first:

- Speak to your bank manager as you may be able to get an agreed overdraft
- Look into Social Fund Loans - these are government-funded, interest-free loans available to those on low incomes
- Check out your local credit union.

If you have no alternative to a payday loan make sure:

- You fully understand the costs and charges involved as rates higher than 1,000% APR are common

- You do not borrow more than you can repay or for longer than necessary. If you miss the repayment, the cost of borrowing even a small amount can become very high, very quickly
- If consumers find themselves relying on payday loans regularly they may find it useful to re-examine their household budget.

Changes to payday loan regulation

On 1st April, 2014, the FCA (Financial Conduct Authority) took over regulation of the consumer credit market from the OFT (Office of Fair Trading). One of the first things the FCA did was to crack down on lenders that offer 'High Cost Short Term Credit' (HCSTC), and this includes payday loans. The key changes include:

Limiting the number of times a loan can be rolled over

Currently if you can't afford to repay your payday loan on time you can usually roll it over to the next month. This flexibility comes as a cost and can quickly lead to a small short term loan turning into a hefty loan term debt.

Usually the balance of your loan is extended by a month, with extra interest and roll over fees whacked on to your borrowing. You generally only have to pay the interest charges upfront when you roll over a loan - but sometimes this can be rolled over as well.

Under FCA rules you will only be able to roll over your loan twice before the balance will be due. This protects you from spiralling debts, while still maintaining some flexibility should you need to extend a loan due to exceptional circumstances. Notably the FCA have chosen to go further than the voluntary Good Practice Charter introduced in 2012, which sets a limit of roll overs to 3.

Stopping lenders from trying to collect payment more than twice

Most payday lenders will use a CPA (Continuous Payment Authority) to collect payment. This is a way of taking money from your bank account that gives the lender the right to take payment on any date they like, and any amount they like. This is important because although lenders should let you know when they plan to take payment and how much it'll be, not all do.

CPAs can be a quick and flexible way to pay your bills as they help you avoid default and late payment charges if the lender tries to collect payment from your account and the money isn't there. However, there is growing concern that they are open to misuse, leading to payday lenders taking money from their customers' accounts without warning. This causes problems if money is taken ahead of other bills, causing defaults on more important debts like your council tax, utilities, mortgage or rent; and leading to bank charges and future credit issues. Under the new FCA rules, lenders will be limited to only two failed CPA attempts. This means that they can't continually try to withdraw money from your account when you don't have the funds available, and instead will need to contact you to find out what's going on. This limit can be reset if you decide to refinance or roll over your loan and pay the amount you currently owe.

Banning part payments by CPA

As well as introducing a limit on the number of times lenders can try to collect payment via CPA, they'll also be limited to how much they're able to collect. In addition, caps were introduced from 2nd january 2015 which limits the amount of interest that can be charged. They are as follows:

- Initial cap of 0.8% a day in interest charges. Someone who takes out a loan of £100 over 30 days, and pays back on time, will therefore pay no more than £24 in interest
- A cap of £15 on the one-off default fee. Borrowers who fail to pay back on time can be charged a maximum of £15, plus a maximum of 0.8% a day in interest and fees
- Total cost cap of 100%. If a borrower defaults, the interest on the debt will build up, but he or she will never have to pay back more than twice the amount they borrowed

Personal loans

Shop around for the best value. Always consider how long it will take you to pay back the loan and how much you will pay in total, as well as how much your monthly payments are. Always check the Annual Percentage Rate (APR) being charged. It is the best way of comparing one deal with another. Generally, the lower the APR, the better the deal.

What to do if you have a complaint

Even if you think the goods are faulty, don't stop your payments or you could end up in trouble. See the shop manager at once and let your finance company know about the problem. If you can't sort it out yourself you should ask for advice from Consumerline on 0300 123 6262, your local Advice Centre or Citizens Advice. You can also get debt advice from the agencies shown below.

If at any stage you feel that the lender is generally trading unfairly, the matter can be referred to the Office of Fair Trading which issues credit licences to all authorised lenders.

The Consumer Credit (Advertisements) Regulations

The Consumer Credit (Advertisements) Regulations 2010 (SI 2010/1970) were laid before Parliament on 5 August 2010, and came into force on 1 February 2011. The Regulations extend to all forms of advertising, including in print, on television or radio, on the internet or by way of telephone canvassing. Certain advertisements indicate that the credit is available only to bodies corporate or only for business purposes.

Representative examples

- Where an advertisement contains an interest rate, which will include a reference to 0% credit, or any figure relating to the cost of credit, then a "representative example" must be given within the advertisement. It will therefore no longer be possible to quote an interest rate within an advertisement without triggering the requirement to display a representative example.

The standard information to be included in a representative example comprises:

- the total amount of credit;

- the rate of interest, and whether that rate is fixed or variable;
- the nature and amount of any charge included in the total charge for credit;
- the representative APR (except in advertisements for authorised non-business overdrafts);
- the cash price of goods and any advance payment (where appropriate); and
- unless the agreement is open ended, the length of the agreement, the total amount payable and the amount of each repayment of credit (where appropriate).
- Note that other rates of interest and charges may be included in the advertisement, but these must be separate from the representative example and less prominent.
- The official guidance issued by BIS in relation to the new Regulations in August 2010 states that where the credit agreement provides for interest to be compounded, then the equivalent annual rate ("EAR") of interest should be shown, rather than a simple rate of interest.
- The representative APR should be denoted as "%APR", accompanied by the word "representative" and where the APR is subject to change be accompanied by the word "variable".
- The Regulations provide that a "representative APR" is the APR at, or below, which the advertiser reasonably expects credit to be provided under at least 51% of the consumer credit agreements entered into as a result of the advertisement. This differs from the current typical APR requirement which is based

on the highest APR that at least 66% of the borrowers accepting credit as a result of the advertisement are given.

- The Regulations require all the standard information to be set out in a clear and concise way and to be accompanied by the words "representative example". All the information should be presented together and must be given equal prominence. The information must be given greater prominence than any other information which triggers the inclusion of the representative APR, for example, the cost of the credit.

- Prominence requires the standard information to stand out from any other information relating to the cost of credit. It should be easily legible. The Regulations do not require any particular font size.

- In respect of running-account credit or where the amount of credit is not known, the representative APR should be based on £1200 (or where the credit is definitely less than that amount, an amount equal to the limit).

- Other than in certain limited circumstances, such as radio or TV advertisements, or those on the premises of the creditor, the advertisement must specify a postal address at which the advertiser may be contacted.

Indicators and incentives

- There are some circumstances where a representative example is not required, other than general advertising with no interest rates or indications of cost. Where an advertisement contains either:

- ○ indicators that credit is available to "non-status" borrowers, or
- ○ comparative indicators that credit is available on more favourable terms than credit offered by the advertiser or other credit providers, or includes incentives to apply for credit

then, **provided** that the advertisement states the representative APR and no other interest rate or amount relating to the cost of credit, it does not need to include the standard information by way of a representative example, nor a postal address for the advertiser. The representative APR in this instance must be of greater prominence than the indicators or incentives.

Security

- Any credit advertisement that requires security to be granted must specify that security is or may be required and must state the nature of that security.

Unlike the 2004 Regulations no wording is prescribed for this and there are no requirements concerning prominence. The information must however be clear and easily legible.

Restrictions on certain expressions

- The Regulations retain other features of the existing UK advertising regime, such as restrictions on the use of certain expressions, for example, "overdraft", "interest free", "loan guaranteed", "gift" etc, other than where these expressions are appropriate given the nature of the credit on offer.

Commencement and transitional arrangements

- The 2010 Advertisement Regulations came into force on 1 February 2011. They apply to credit advertisements published on or after 1 February 2011, or which continue to be published after that date, subject to some limited transitional provisions.

Breach

Breach of the Regulations is an offence, and persistent breaches may be considered by the OFT when it considers any application to renew a consumer credit license.

Main Credit agencies in the UK

There are a number of credit agencies in the UK. The most well known are:

Experian

Consumer Help Service

PO Box 9000

Nottingham NG80 7WF

Tel: 0800 013 8888

Equifax Ltd

Customer Service Centre

PO Box 10036 Leicester

LE3 4FS

www.equifax.co.uk 0113 380 8000

You can write to the above any time and ask to see the information they have on you. You can also order your file online and over the telephone from Equifax and Experian so long as you have a credit or debit card in your own name.

If you write you will need to send a fee, usually £25, give full name address and date of birth, include any other address that you have had within the last six years, give your business name and address if you are a sole trader or partnership. Keep copies of any letters that you send. The agency must reply within seven working days to ask for any more information from you, tell you that it does not have a file on you or send you the file.

If a lender or other turns you down for a loan, you can check the information that has been provided. You can ask for the name of the credit reference agency that provided information about you if:

- You write to the lender within 28 days of your last contact about the credit deal
- The lender used a credit agency, they must tell you the agency's name and address within seven working days of your letter.

There are several organisations that will assist if you have a specific complaint against a lender. they are listed below.

The Consumer Credit Association (CCA)
The CCA represents over 75% of firms that provide unsecured loans in the home credit industry. The CCA has a code of practice which its

members must comply with, as well as a business conduct pledge. The CCA also has internal conciliation and arbitration schemes to help resolve complaints made against its members. They can be contacted as follows:

Consumer Credit Association
1 Minerva Court
Minerva Avenue
Chester
CH1 4QT
Telephone: 01244 394760
email: complaints@ccauk.org
Website: www.ccauk.org

Consumer Credit Trade Association

The CCTA represents credit lenders including finance houses, retailers and building societies. The CCTA has a code of practice with which its members must comply. The CCTA has an internal conciliation scheme to resolve complaints made against its members. there is also an independent arbitration scheme, run by the Chartered Institute of Arbitrators.

The CCTA can be contacted as follows:

Unit G5, Spring Mill,
Main Street, Wilsden,
West Yorkshire, BD15 0DX
01274 714 959
email: info@ccta.co.uk
Website: www.ccta.co.uk

The Finance and Leasing Association (FLA)

The FLA represents the UK and finance leasing industry, including creditors offering hire purchase and conditional sale agreements, secured and unsecured loans, credit cards and store cards. The FLA has a code of practice with which all its full members must comply. The FLA has an independent arbitration scheme for consumer complaints which is run by the Chartered Institute of Arbitrators. The contact details are as follows:

Finance and Leasing Association
2nd Floor Imperial House
15-19 Kingsway
London
WC2B 4AS
Tel: 020 7836 6511
email: info@ fla.org.uk
Website: www.fla.org.uk

****

Chapter 11

The Consumer Protection from Unfair Trading Regulations 2008, as amended.

Trade Descriptions-Misleading Prices-Aggressive Selling and General Unfair Practices

The Consumer Protection from Unfair Trading Regulations 2008 (known as the CPRs) cover commercial practices between traders and consumers - 'acts, omissions, course of conduct, representation or commercial communication (including advertising and marketing) by a trader, which is directly connected with the promotion, sale or supply of a product to or from consumers, whether occurring before, during or after a commercial transaction (if any) in relation to a product'. Note: a 'product' is any goods or service, and includes rights and obligations. The 2008 Act was amended by new regulations introduced in 2014. These amendments are outlined at the end of the chapter.

The legislation

The Consumer Protection from Unfair Trading Regulations 2008 came into force on 26 May 2008 and implemented the European Union-wide Unfair Commercial Practices Directive (UCPD). The aim of the UCPD is to harmonise consumer protection laws across the European Union to prevent business practices that are unfair to consumers and all Member States are introducing equivalent legislation. The Regulations replace a lot of consumer protection legislation, including Part III of the Consumer Protection Act 1987 (which dealt with misleading prices), the majority of the Trade Descriptions Act 1968, and the Control of Misleading Advertising Regulations 1988.

What is prohibited?

Effectively the CPRs prohibit trading practices that are unfair to consumers. There are four different types of practices to consider:

1. Practices prohibited in all circumstances
2. Misleading actions and omissions
3. Aggressive practices
4. General duty not to trade unfairly

For the last three practice types above it is necessary to show that the action of the trader has an effect (or is likely to have an effect) on the actions of the consumer. There does not have to be a physical consumer as this is a test looking at how the average consumer is - or is likely to be - affected. The CPRs identify three different types of consumer:

- average consumer
- targeted consumer
- vulnerable consumer

...recognising that different types of consumers may react to a practice in different ways.

1. Practices prohibited in all circumstances

Schedule 1 to the CPRs (PDF 195KB) introduces 31 practices that are always considered to be unfair and therefore are banned in all circumstances.

These include:

False endorsements/authorisation

- false claims of membership of trade associations claiming a product has been approved by a public or private body when it has not.

Misleading avaiability

- bait advertising (or 'bait and switch') where a trader lures a consumer into believing he can buy a product at a low price when the trader is aware he does not have reasonable stock available or is not able to supply at that price, or attempts to 'sell-up' to a higher priced product
- falsely stating a product is only available for a very limited time in order to make the consumer make an immediate decision

Misleading context/effect

- claiming a trader is going to cease trading or move premises when he is not (for example, bogus closing down sales)
- falsely claiming a product has curative properties

- describing a product as 'free', 'gratis', 'without charge' or similar if a consumer is going to have to pay more than the cost of responding to the advertisement and collecting or paying for delivery of the item
- including an invoice or similar in marketing material, implying a consumer has ordered the product when he has not
- failing to make it clear that a person is actually a trader or creating the impression he is a consumer (for example, failing to indicate trade status when selling a second-hand car)
- creating the impression that a product can legally be sold, when in fact, it cannot

Pyramid schemes

- operating or promoting such schemes are specifically prohibited, provided they fit within the definition of a pyramid scheme (that is, a scheme where a consumer gives consideration for the opportunity to receive compensation that is derived primarily from the introduction of other consumers into the scheme, rather than from the sale or consumption of products)

Prize draws

- competitions where the prizes described (or equivalent) are not awarded
- creating the false impression that a consumer has won, or will win, a prize when there is no prize or claiming the prize is subject to the consumer paying money or incurring a cost

Agressive sales

- creating the impression a consumer can't leave the premises until a contract is formed visiting a consumer at home and refusing to leave when asked to leave (except when the trader has a legal right to enforce a contractual obligation)
- making persistent and unwanted solicitations by phone/fax/email (except when a trader has a legal right to enforce a contractual obligation)
- making a direct exhortation to children to buy a product or to persuade their parents to buy a product for them (pester power)
- telling a consumer a trader's job will be in jeopardy if the consumer does not buy the product

Unreasonable demands

- requiring a consumer who wishes to claim on an insurance policy to produce irrelevant documents or failing to respond to correspondence in order to dissuade the consumer from exercising his contractual rights

2. Misleading actions and omissions

The CPRs prohibit misleading actions and misleading omissions that cause, or are likely to cause, the average consumer to take a different transactional decision - that is, any decision taken by the consumer concerning the purchasing of the product or whether to exercise a contractual right in relation to the product, including decisions not to act. This does not only relate to pre-shopping but includes after-sales and continues for the lifetime of the product.

MISLEADING ACTIONS (REGULATION 5)

This regulation prohibits giving false information to, or deceiving, consumers. A misleading action occurs when a practice misleads through the information it contains, or its deceptive presentation, and causes, or is likely to cause, the average consumer to take a different transactional decision.

There are three different types of misleading actions:

- misleading information generally (see below)
- creating confusion with competitors' products
- failing to honour commitments made in a code of conduct

The information that may be considered as misleading is very wide, and is listed in the legislation itself, including such things as:

- the existence or nature of the product
- the main characteristics of the product - for example, the benefits of the product or the geographical origin
- the price or the manner in which it is calculated
- the need for a service, part, replacement or repair
- the nature, attributes and rights of the trader - such as qualifications

MISLEADING OMISSIONS (REGULATION 6)

This regulation prohibits giving insufficient information about a product. It is a breach of the CPRs to fail to give consumers the information they need to make an informed choice in relation to a product if this would cause, or be likely to cause, the average consumer to take a different transactional decision.

A trader is required to give consumers material information, that is the information the average consumer needs, according to the context, to make an informed choice. It is a breach of the CPRs:

- to omit material information
- to hide material information
- to provide material information in a manner that is unclear, unintelligible, ambiguous or untimely
- to fail to identify the commercial intent (unless this is apparent from the context)

3. Aggressive practices (regulation 7)

The CPRs prohibit aggressive commercial practices that intimidate or exploit consumers, restricting their ability to make free or informed choices. In order for an aggressive practice to be unfair it must cause, or be likely to cause, the average consumer to take a different transactional decision. A commercial practice is aggressive if:

- it significantly impairs, or is likely to significantly impair, the average consumer's freedom of choice or conduct in relation to the product through the use of harassment, coercion or undue influence, and
- it thereby causes him to take a different transactional decision

To decide whether a practice breaches this regulation, account shall be taken of:

- timing, location, nature or persistence

- use of threatening or abusive language or behaviour
- exploitation by the trader of any specific misfortune or circumstance that impairs the consumer's judgement, in order to influence the consumer's decision with regard to the product
- any onerous or disproportionate non-contractual barrier imposed by the trader where a consumer wishes to exercise rights under the contract (for example, rights to terminate the contract or switch to another product or trader)
- any threat to take action that cannot legally be taken
- Note: 'coercion' includes the use of physical force, and 'undue influence' means exploiting a position of power in relation to the consumer so as to apply pressure, even without the use of (or threatening to use) physical force, in a way that significantly limits the consumer's ability to make an informed decision.

4. General duty not to trade unfairly (regulation 3)

This is effectively failing to act in accordance with reasonable expectations of acceptable trading practice. Regulations 3(1) and 3(3) set out a general prohibition of unfair business to consumer practices and will allow action to be taken in relation to unfair practices which do not fit into the more specific prohibitions. This will cover a wide range of unfair practices including practices which may emerge in the future. The general prohibition prohibits practices that:

- contravene the requirements of professional diligence (defined as the standard of special skill and care that a trader may reasonably be expected to exercise towards consumers which is commensurate with either honest market practice in the trader's field of activity, or the general principle of good faith in the trader's field of activity)
- materially distort the economic behaviour of the average consumer (or are likely to) with regard to the product (that is, appreciably to impair the average consumer's ability to make an informed decision thereby causing him to take a transactional decision that he would not have taken otherwise)

What are the consequences of non-compliance?

Enforcers may take civil enforcement action in respect of a breach of the CPRs under Part 8 of the Enterprise Act 2002. This can be done by applying to a court for an enforcement order and a breach of any order could lead to up to two years' imprisonment and/or an unlimited fine. The CPRs also contain criminal offences that can be prosecuted by the Office of Fair Trading (OFT), trading standards services, or the Department of Enterprise, Trade & Investment in Northern Ireland (and by the Lord Advocate in Scotland). The penalties are:

- on summary conviction, a fine not exceeding the statutory maximum (currently £5,000)
- on conviction on indictment, an unlimited fine or imprisonment for up to two years (or both)

Amendments to the 2008 regulations

As of 1st October 2014 amendments were made to the Regulations which give the consumer new rights to redress - if they have been the victim of a misleading action - for example a false statement - or aggressive selling.

These break down into three key areas:

A right to undo the contract A person will have 90 days to end the contract and get a refund. The 90-day time limit will start on the latest of when:

- they entered into the contract
- they first received the goods, services or digital content
- the lease began (if the contract is a lease), or
- the right of cancellation is first exercisable.

A person can only receive a refund if they haven't fully consumed goods or digital products, or received a service in full. This is also on the provision that any goods supplied are made available for collection by the trader.

It's important to note that if a person took out finance to pay for a contract that was made as a result of misleading or aggressive selling, they can get out of the contract and recoup anything that they have paid.

A right to a discount on the price paid A person will be able to seek a discount in respect of past or future payments due under a contract. For contracts worth £5,000 or less, the Regulations entitle the consumer to a 25%, 50%, 75% or 100% discount on the payments depending on whether the trader's breach is considered to be minor, significant, serious or very serious. For contracts worth over £5,000, a person is entitled to a discount to the extent that the contract price exceeded the market price.

The level of seriousness of the trader's actions will depend on their behaviour, the impact this has had on them and how long it has been since they signed the contract. If a consumer chooses to receive a discount, they cannot then cancel the contract: they have to choose one remedy or the other.

An entitlement to seek damages If a person incurs a financial loss that they wouldn't have done if it weren't for the trader's actions, they will be able to make a claim for damages. They can make a claim for damages as well as choosing to receive a discount or cancel the contract.

A claim can also be made if they have suffered alarm, distress or physical inconvenience or discomfort as a result of the trader's actions.

Be aware that traders have a defence to many of the offences set out in the Regulations if they can demonstrate that their actions were due to an accident, a mistake, the act or default of another person, information supplied by another person, or factors outside of their control. However, they can only rely on this defence if they took reasonable precautions and exercised all due diligence to avoid committing the offence.

Important factors to note:

A person must have entered into a contract For these new rights to redress to apply, they must have entered into a contract. This is different from the rest of the regulations where it is enough to show they took some other kind of transactional decision, like going into a shop because of a misleading ad in the window.

Miss-leading action must be a significant factor If a person entered into a contract as a result of a misleading action or aggressive selling, they will need to show that this was at least a significant factor in their decision to enter into the contract. Misleading omissions are not covered These new rights to redress do not apply to misleading omissions.

****

Chapter 12

Unsafe Goods

Sometimes the consumer purchases a good which, when tested, turns out to be unsafe. If a contract exists between the consumer and retailer then the Consumer Rights Act 2015 will give protection. If no such contract exists then the Consumer Protection Act will apply.

The Consumer Protection Act 1987 also provides for criminal liability. The claim must be made within three years of the date the damage was caused, or three years from the date the damage could reasonably have been discovered. The manufacturers or importers liability ends ten years after the goods first appeared on the market.

The Consumer Protection Act is not aimed at shoddy goods, but at unsafe goods. The Act sets out a general offence of supplying consumer goods which are not reasonably safe, provides for safety regulations to be made for products and provides for a system of notices to assist trading standards officers to enforce the Act.

Many consumer goods are controlled, or the safety of goods is controlled by detailed regulations related to the manufacture of a particular good. However, the Consumer Protection Act provides for a general safety standard. Section 19 of the Act defines what is "safe" and states: 'Safe' in relation to any goods means that there is no risk, or no risk apart from one reduced to a minimum. Therefore, goods do not have to be 100% safe'. This is probably an impossibility. However, the risk of unsafe goods must be reduced to a minimum.

A person is guilty of an offence if he supplies any consumer goods which fail to comply with the general safety requirement, offers or agrees to supply any such good or exposes or possesses any such goods for supply. Section 10 (1) and (2) are the relevant sections of the Act and section 10(2) contains a list of factors to be taken into account.

There are, as with all areas of law, recognised defences to the supply of unsafe goods. The important ones are:

a) the goods conform in a relevant respect with a European Community obligation;

b) the goods conform to any applicable safety regulations or safety standards set out by the Secretary of State for Trade and Industry for the purpose of the general safety requirement

c) that the offenders reasonably believed that the goods would not be used or consumed in the United Kingdom;

d) that the goods were supplied in the course of a business and that at the time the retailer did not know or had no reasonable grounds for believing that the goods failed to comply with the general safety requirements.;

e) that the goods were not supplied as new. The general safety requirement does not apply to second hand goods.

Penalties for contravention of the law can be up to £5,000 fine or six months in prison. However, this can vary greatly and a trader on trial for manslaughter can expect a higher sentence. In addition to the above, the General Product Safety Regulations 2005 give a consumer protection against the sale or manufacture of goods that are unsafe.

You do not have to have been injured by the goods for an offence to have been committed. Most new, second-hand and reconditioned goods are covered by these regulations unless there is a specific European safety law that applies.

The European Community has been very active in this area and the current position (check for position post BREXIT) is that a General Product Safety Directive has been issued to standardise the safety of food throughout Europe and was introduced onto the Statute books in 1999. Also, the Toy Safety (1995)Regulations 1995, based on a European Directive, governs the safety of toys and will give specific information on what constitutes a safe toy. If you feel any product is unsafe you should contact The Citizens Advice Consumer Service on 03454 04 05 06.

****

Chapter 13
Package Holidays

Now, in 2020 and 2021, the travel industry is in a mess and many people who had purchased holidays, package or other, have been trying to obtain refunds. In many cases, these refunds have been made but a few larger companies are still lagging behind in their legal obligation to pay. At the end of this chapter there is an outline of rights and responsibilities of tour companies and airlines during the pandemic.

There are various common law protections in the case of holidays. However, the main area of consumer protection in the case of package holidays are the Package Travel, Package Holidays and Package Tours Regulations 1992 and the ABTA Code of practice.

The Regulations were introduced to comply with EU Directive 90/314 on Package Holidays and Package Tours. The directive was inevitable because of the level of tourism across EU member states. Most consumer problems related to holidays concern differences between the holiday description on booking and the actual reality. It is possible in these circumstances that there is also an offence under s14 Trade Descriptions Act 1978.

Package travel regulations 2018
From 1 July 2018, the Package Travel Directive came into force, extending consumer protection beyond traditional package holidays organised by tour operators. The liability of package organisers has

not changed significantly under the new directive, but many travel companies may face such liability for the first time due to the widened definition of a 'package'. Under the new directive, companies that put together a package for a customer will be responsible for all the services included as part of the package. This means that agents who put together a flight and a hotel, for example, will have the same responsibilities as traditional package-holiday organisers.

The Package Travel, Package Holidays and Package Tours Regulations 1992 (as amended)

The definition of 'package holidays'.

The Regulations do not alter the existing common-law protections but add significant duties on tour operators. The Regulations apply to all package holidays-but the word `package' is given a very broad definition in Regulation 2 (1): the prearranged combination of at least two of the following components when sold or offered for sale at an inclusive price and when the service covers a period of more than 24 hours or includes overnight accommodation:

1) transport
2) accommodation
3) c)other tourist services not ancillary to transport or
4) accommodation and accounting for a significant proportion of the package and submission of separate accounts for different components shall not cause the arrangement to be other than a package

5) the fact that a combination is arranged at the request of the consumer in accordance with his specific instructions (whether modified or not) shall not of itself cause it to be treated as other than prearranged,

Information to be given by the holiday operator before the contract is concluded

The basic common law rules on formation can apply. The brochure is generally seen as an invitation to treat. But the Regulations, in Regulation 9, provide certain safeguards by ensuring that certain information is given to the consumer before the contract is concluded, and that the information is comprehensible to the consumer.

The necessary information is detailed in schedule 2:

- the intended destination
- the intended means of travel
- the exact dates and the place of departure
- the locality of accommodation and its classification
- meals that are included in the package
- the minimum number of travellers to allow the holiday to go ahead
- any relevant itineraries, visits or excursions
- the names and full addresses of the organiser, retailer and insurer
- the price and any details with regard to revising the price

- the payment schedule and method of payment
- any other necessary details, such as specific arrangements for diet etc, that have been indicated by the consumer
- the method and period for complaints to be made.

This information must be given to the consumer both before the contract is made and in the contract itself. This will not apply to late bookings. Failure to comply is a breach under regulation 9(3) and the operator is then prevented from relying on terms that are not sufficiently explained in this way - and the consumer may also cancel the holiday.

Statements made in holiday brochures

The common law distinction between terms and `trade puffs' applies where no reasonable person could rely on the statement. But, in any case, by regulation 4, holiday operators will be liable if they supply misleading information in their descriptive matter.

Liability
Terms and performance of the contract

By regulation 15(1) the operator is liable for the improper performance of the contract by other service providers. The only exception is where the improper performance is neither the fault of the operator nor of any other service provider:

- including where it is the fault of the consumer

- or where it is caused by the unforeseeable and unavoidable act of the third party; and
- where forces majeure applies, e.g. hurricanes
- The ABTA Code of Practice also requires that it should be a term of all contracts for package holidays that the operator will accept liability for the acts or omissions of their employees, agents, sub-contractors and suppliers which results in death, injury or illness-and that the operators will offer advice, guidance and financial assistance of up to £5000 to consumers on holiday who suffer death, injury or illness.

Alterations to the holiday

Alteration depends on the terms of the contract-a common term allows alteration to the itinerary. If an alteration amounts to non-performance then it is a breach of the contract by the operator and will be classed as a breach of the condition allowing the consumer to repudiate and claim back the cost of the holiday.

The ABTA Code Clause 2.4 requires operators to offer suitable alternatives in the case of cancellation or alteration.

Overbooking of flights

Passengers who are denied travel because of overbooking are entitled to a choice/combination of:

- reimbursement of the cost of the ticket
- re-routing to the destination at the earliest moment
- re-routing at a later date, at the passengers convenience
- compensation

There are special rules applying to overbooked flights from airports in the European Union. The rules also apply to flights from airports outside the EU but flying into an EU airport, on an EU airline.

These rules apply only if you were not allowed to board the flight, not if you volunteered to take a different flight. You must have a valid ticket and have met check in deadlines at the airport. If these conditions are met then you will be entitled to a full refund of your ticket and a free return flight to your first point of departure, if needed, or another flight either as soon as possible or at a later date of your choice. You will also be entitled to:

- compensation. The amount you get will depend on the circumstances, i.e. how late you were as a result of the overbooking
- compensation for two telephone calls, e mails or other forms of communication
- reasonable meals and refreshments if you have to wait for a later flight
- Hotel accommodation if appropriate (stay overnight until next flight)

If the above EU rules don't apply then you should check the terms and conditions with the operator.

Remember, the law applies to this area as it does to all other areas and the operator cannot opt out. If you are not satisfied with what has happened then you should contact ABTA who run an arbitration scheme (address at the back of the book).

You can also contact the Association of Independent Tour Operators on www.abta.com.

Insolvency of the tour operator

The Package Travel, Package Holidays and package Tours Regulations 1992 apply. Under regulation 16(1) tour operators must at all times be able to satisfy evidence of sufficient funds to be able to return deposits in the event of insolvency. Consumers who pay by credit card are also protected under the Consumer Credit Act 1974.

ABTA bonding arrangements ensure that a consumer is not left stranded when a tour operator goes into insolvency during his/her holidays.

Remedies

Damages are usually awarded on the basis of difference in value between what was contracted for and what was provided. Incidental losses are also possible. Claims are also possible for physical discomfort. Operators are, basically, liable for all losses that arise from the breach.

Recent developments in the law

The Office of Fair Trading issued guidance to tour operators on March 2004. The OFT believes that many standard form terms in contracts fall short of the requirements of the Unfair Contract terms In Consumer Contract Regulations 1999 and has suggested alternative wording for operators to avoid liability. These include:

- standard terms on responsibility for errors and changes in invoices or brochures,

- the acceptance of responsibility for statements made by agents, employees and representatives
- Right to transfer holidays when prevented from travelling
- Price revision clauses
- Rights on cancellation and alteration
- The right to compensation and the amount of compensation
- Cancellation by the consumer
- Cancellation charges for failure to pay deposit of balance
- Rights where services not supplied during the holiday
- Exclusion of liability
- Reporting of complaints
- 'Read and understand' declarations

Flights watchdog orders airlines to end passenger name change rip-off

The aviation regulator is preparing to crack down on airlines that charge up to £160 to change a name on a ticket amid warnings that too many passengers are being stung by hidden costs. The Civil Aviation Authority (CAA) will order airlines to rewrite confusing booking rules to prevent travellers paying a "significant amount of money" to correct a simple mistake.

Consumer advice concerning travel and refunds during the pandemic

These are extraordinary times and a lot of confusion and distress has been caused due to the effect of the pandemic on travellers and airlines and other travel customers. Although we have outlined the law above, the details below might help to clarify important issues.

Getting money back for a cancelled holiday because of coronavirus
You can get money back as long as it was a package holiday. If your holiday company cancels for any reason, including the lockdown in England from 5 November to 2 December, it will have to give you a full refund. Some companies are providing refunds much more quickly than others. And unfortunately some are ignoring this requirement altogether and are refusing to reimburse customers.

Accepting a Refund Credit Note
Refund Credit Notes were introduced as a sort of IOU to help travel companies avoid a cash-flow crisis when they were forced to refund so many holidays at the same time. The government has promised to protect RCNs issued up to 31 December 2020, so if the travel company fails, customers with credit notes will get their money back from the Atol scheme. The Civil Aviation Authority, which manages Atol, says the credit notes must be redeemed for a new holiday or refunded by 30 September 2021. Credit notes might be an attractive option if your travel company is offering you additional credit as an incentive, but the law says you are entitled to a full cash refund if you prefer. Don't accept a credit note if you have any concerns.

If your package holiday was cancelled, you don't have to accept a refund credit note, nor do you have to rebook. You are legally entitled to a refund. Make this clear to the firm, in writing. If it still won't do the right thing, you could try to claim through your card provider. The company that took your money is responsible for issuing your refund – so if you booked with a third party agent, go direct to them.

Do airlines issue refunds?

If your flight is cancelled by the airline, you're due a refund. This applies for all flights on any airline that departs from an EU country, as well as Iceland, Norway, Switzerland and the UK, and flights on any EU carrier from any airport. Outside of the EU, the rules are more complex. Your rights likely depend on the individual airline or travel agent's terms and conditions.

Those who have tried to claim a refund online say they've accidentally been sent a voucher instead and, once issued, BA is refusing to exchange vouchers for cash. Ryanair automatically issues customers with vouchers, which they can then exchange for cash. Although it claims to have made rapid progress in processing refunds, some customers say they are still waiting months. EasyJet customers can claim refunds online and it appears to be processing most (but not all) refunds within 30 days.

If your flight is cancelled, you are due a refund. You don't have to request a refund before your flight's scheduled departure. In fact you have at least 12 months to make a claim. If the airline websites aren't working, or you can't reach the carrier to request a refund, your options are to keep trying or to try to claim through your debit or credit card provider, or paypal.

Can I claim a refund if the Airline hasn't cancelled my flight?
Unfortunately not. Even when there are FCDO travel warnings or a nationwide lockdown in place, airlines will not necessarily cancel flights. This is despite the fact that holidaymakers taking those flights will invalidate their travel insurance, unless they have specialist cover.

Refunds on accommodation
Airbnb, Booking.com, Expedia and some major hotel chains waived their cancellation fees for those whose travel plans have had to be abandoned because of the outbreak. However, those booking after coronavirus was a 'known event' were encouraged to choose accommodation with a flexible booking policy. If your hotel has closed, you're due a full refund. Even if it is open but government restrictions prevent you from getting to your accommodation, CMA advice suggests you should be entitled to a refund.

UK holiday cottages
Unlike with flights and package holidays, you're not necessarily entitled to a refund if your holiday cottage booking is cancelled due to coronavirus. It depends on the terms and conditions in your booking contract. If your contract states that you're entitled to your money back if the company you booked with cancels the booking, then that's what you should demand. If a national lockdown or local coronavirus restrictions prevent you from travelling, such as Tier 3 restrictions in England and local lockdowns in parts of Wales, you should be entitled to a full refund.

Travel on ferries

If you're booked on a ferry service that's been cancelled, the provider is obligated to offer a choice between an alternative journey or a full refund. However, some companies are currently issuing vouchers instead. If your ferry journey has been cancelled you'll probably be issued with a voucher, rather than a refund.

If you're unhappy about this, try contacting the ferry company directly to ask for your money back. If the service hasn't been cancelled but you don't want to go you can usually amend the booking, but cancelling it will incur a fee.

Cancelling a trip

If you cancel your trip you risk losing what you've already paid, but some travel companies have introduced more flexible rebooking policies. But in the event that these holidays are later cancelled, you'll have given up your right to a cash refund, so it might be better to wait for the operator to cancel. The same applies to flights. If you cancel your flight before the airline cancels, you won't be entitled to a refund.

Airlines are only obliged to give passengers two weeks' notice of cancellations before they're obliged to pay compensation for the inconvenience (unless there are exceptional circumstances, such as government flight bans), so you might have to wait until 14 days before the departure date to find out if your flight is going ahead.

Travel insurance and Coronavirus

Major travel insurers responded to the pandemic by changing policies so they no longer covered coronavirus-related incidents, but over the past few months at least two dozen insurers have reintroduced some form of coronavirus cover. However, there is a big difference between policies in terms of what is actually covered. It's important to check your policy to see if you're covered for medical bills if you get sick with coronavirus, or if you have to cancel because of government restrictions, if you get coronavirus before you travel, or if you're told by Test & Trace to self-isolate. Most standard travel policies don't provide cancellation, disruption or abandonment cover if you travel or book a holiday against FCDO advice. There are specialist policies available for these areas, but bear in mind that the advice is there for a reason and you'd be travelling to countries deemed risky by the government.

If you no longer wish to travel due to FCDO advice and you bought your insurance before coronavirus became a known event, you may be able to claim from your insurer for any costs that won't be refunded. Check with your insurer.

Before you get in touch with your insurer, you should try to get a refund from travel or accommodation providers. Insurers will only pay out for costs that couldn't be refunded, so you must explore that route first. If your travel operator tells you to claim on your insurance, get this in writing.

****

Chapter 14

Food Safety

In chapter 13, we looked at the rights of the consumer and unsafe goods. In this chapter we look at the all-important area of food and health and safety.

Food poisoning is an increasing problem in our society and in the last decade there has been a massive increase in the number of reported cases. The major protection for the consumer in this area is the Food Safety Act 1990, as amended by the General Food Regulations 2004. In addition, the Food Safety Act Amendment Regulations 2004 brought the Act in line with EU Regulation EC/178/2002. In England, The Food Safety and Hygiene (England) Regulations 2013 provides for the enforcement of certain provisions of Regulation 178/2002 and for the food hygiene legislation. It also provides national law for: bulk transport by sea of liquid oils or fats and raw sugar; the direct supply by the producer of small quantities of meat from poultry or lagomorphs slaughtered on the farm; temperature control in retail establishments; restrictions on the sales and supply of raw cows' drinking milk and derogations relating to low throughput establishments (slaughterhouses).

The aim of the 1990 Act, as amended, is to control all aspects of food safety throughout the food distribution chain. Breaches of the

Act result in criminal liability. There is an unlimited fine attached to breaches of the Act and also a maximum prison term of two years.

Section 7 of The 1990 Food Safety Act, as amended, creates a specific offence of rendering food injurious to health with the intent that it should be sold for human consumption. The offence can be committed in several ways:

a) by adding any article or substance to the food
b) by using any article or substance as an ingredient in the preparation of food
c) abstracting any constituent from the food;
d) subjecting the food to any other process or treatment.
Section 8 of the Act also creates a number of offences and states:

"Any person who sells for human consumption or offers, exposes or advertises for sale for such consumption or has in his possession for the purpose of such sale or of preparation for such sale any food which fails to comply with food safety requirements shall be guilty of an offence"

Food can be unfit for human consumption even if it poses no health hazard. This is relevant to food which has started to incur mould growth.

The Food Safety Act also deals with food which misleads consumers. Section 14 states that anyone who sells food which is, by substance, not of the nature and quality demanded by the consumer is guilty of an offence, namely that of misleading the consumer. There are many examples here, particularly concerning meat and meat substitutes, i.e., fat instead of mince and fish. Section 15 of the Act Deals with the labelling of food and attempts to mislead by false claims. The Act also contains many powers for food inspectors to inspect and seize food and to close down premises. There are, as with the other areas of law, defences to breaches of the Act. One main defence is that of due diligence. However, in common with the other areas, defences have to be sound and backed up with concrete evidence.

The Food Standards Act 1999

The Act was introduced in the House of Commons on 10 June 1999 and received Royal Assent on 11 November 1999.

The main purpose of the Act was to establish the Food Standards Agency, provide it with functions and powers, and to transfer to it certain functions in relation to food safety and standards under other Acts. The Act gives effect to the proposals of the White Paper, 'The Food Standards Agency: A Force for Change' (Cm 3830). It sets out the Agency's main objective of protecting public health in relation to food and the functions that it will assume in pursuit of that aim, and gives the Agency the powers necessary to enable it to act in the consumer's interest at any stage in the food production and supply chain. The Act provides for the Agency's main organisational and accountability arrangements. In addition, it provides powers to establish a scheme for the notification of the results of tests for food-borne diseases.

Other pertinent law is the 2014 Food Standards Regulations which introduced a new regime of Improvement Notices.

****

Chapter 15

Consumer Remedies

There are a number of remedies available to the consumer. The Principal remedy is that through the civil courts-more specifically the small claims court, which is part of the county court. However, before using the small claims court, it may be necessary to consider other remedies, such as an Alternative Dispute Resolution scheme.

These schemes use a third party, such as an arbitrator or an ombudsman to help the consumer and supplier of goods or services to reach a solution. You will usually have to complete the suppliers internal complaints scheme beforehand and a fee may be payable to use the scheme. This is usually refunded if you are successful. Some schemes are legally binding, which means that you can't take court action if you aren't satisfied with the decision, except to enforce an award. If the claim is over £5,000 then the use of ADR should be discussed with a solicitor.

Advantages of ADR
The main advantages are:

- you may resolve your problem
- you may be awarded compensation
- the procedure is less formal than going to court

- in some schemes the decision may be binding on the trader but not on you, leaving you free to pursue further action through the courts
- it may cost less than going to court
- the procedure is confidential
- Some potential disadvantages or points to think about:
- the costs involved. Do a cost comparison before committing to ADR
- would you prefer to have a hearing so that your point can be put across in person
- if the arbitrators decision is legally binding, it will prevent you taking the matter through the courts
- you may have to pay further costs to enforce the arbitrators decision through the courts

Types of ADR
The main types of ADR that deal with consumer disputes are conciliation, arbitration or mediation. They are usually provided by trade associations, if you wish to use one of these schemes you should ask the supplier whether they are members of a trade association and if they are contact the association to find out whether they offer ADR.

Conciliation
In consumer disputes conciliation is the first stage in the arbitration process. The conciliator is usually a member of the trade association. Both the consumer and supplier will be asked to give

written details of the complaint, including evidence and the conciliator will give an opinion on the best solution. Decisions are not binding leaving the way free for court action or arbitration.

Arbitration

Arbitration is a procedure for settling disputes in which both the consumer and the supplier usually agree to accept the decision of the arbitrator as legally binding. This means that court action cannot be taken except to enforce the award if the supplier doesn't pay. The arbitrator will make a decision based on written evidence provided by the supplier and consumer. The decision is confidential. Some contracts for services include an arbitration clause stating that you will refer any dispute to arbitration. Although this is binding once you have signed the agreement, if the total cost is below the small claims limit (£5,000) you cannot be forced to arbitrate unless you gave your agreement after the dispute arose.

Mediation

If a mediation scheme is used, the mediator will help consumer and supplier to negotiate an acceptable agreement and will act as a go between if you don't want to meet. If the supplier agrees to mediation, then both sides will be asked to give details of the dispute, including supplying evidence and will be asked to sign a mediation agreement. This will give the framework for mediation. If an agreement is reached then both sides will be asked to sign a draft terms of settlement. This will be legally binding unless it is stated otherwise. Mediation can be expensive but the Community

Legal Service may provide help under the legal help scheme or the public funded legal representation scheme, depending on your circumstances.

Ombudsman schemes

Many services have an Ombudsman scheme that can be used by the consumer. Many financial services, for example, are covered by an Ombudsman scheme. You will only be able to refer the matter to the Ombudsman after you have exhausted the supplier's internal complaints scheme.

The Ombudsman will make a recommendation or ruling, usually accepted by the supplier but which is not legally binding. However, a court will take an Ombudsman's ruling into account when making a decision. All Ombudsman's schemes are free.

Locating an ADR scheme

If you wish to pursue ADR then the first action is to find out whether the trader is a member of a trade association that offers such a service. If you experience any difficulty then you should contact Citizens Advice on 03454 04 05 06. The Law Society also has a Civil and Commercial Mediation Panel to help members of the public find qualified solicitor mediators. To obtain more details about this panel phone 0207 320 5650. For further help you should contact the Chartered Institute of Arbitrators, 12 Bloomsbury Square, London WC1A 2LP Tel 020 7421 7444. If, for whatever reason it is not possible to resolve the dispute through ADR, then it may be necessary to pursue the case through the small claims court.

What follows is a description of the small claims procedure and of remedies available to the aggrieved consumer. Following this there will be a description of other remedies, such as the office of fair-trading.

The Small Claims Court

The first fact to be aware of when taking a trader to court in order to obtain some sort of compensation is that it is not necessary to have either legal knowledge or use a solicitor when using the small claims procedure in the County Court.

Commencing a claim

A person can start legal action in any court and if the case is defended the court will decide what procedure to use. If the case is a simple one, with a value of £5000 or less, the court will decide that the small claims procedure will be used and will allocate the case to the small claims track. In most cases, the court will not order that costs are paid by the losing party in a small claims case. For this reason, most people do not use a solicitor when making a small claim. It may, however, be possible to get legal help using the legal help scheme.

Types of case dealt with in the small claims track

When the court is considering whether to allocate the case to a small claims track it will take into account a number of factors, but the main factor is the value of the case.

If the value of a case is £5000 or less it will generally be allocated to the small claims track. However, if it is a personal injury claim, it will be allocated to the small claims track only if the value of the claim for the personal injuries is not more than £1000. If the claimant is a tenant and is claiming against their landlord because repairs are needed to the premises and the cost of the work is £1000 or less, the case will be allocated to the small claims track.

Types of claims in the small claims court

The most common types of small claims are:

- Compensation for faulty goods, for example washing machines or other goods that go wrong
- Compensation for faulty services provided, for example by builders, garages and so on
- Disputes between landlords and tenants, for examples, rent arrears, compensation for not doing repairs
- Wages owed or money in lieu of notice

If a case proves to be too complex then a judge may refer the case to another track for a full hearing, even if below the limit for that track.

Actions before applying to court

Before applying to court it is always necessary to try to solve the problem amicably, or as amicably as possible without recourse to legal action. We have already discussed ADR. A person who intends to commence a claim should write a 'letter before action' which should set out terms for settlement before applying to court.

For example, if a television is defective, or workmanship on a car is faulty, there is no point applying to court for compensation before contacting the garage or repair shop. Whilst this may seem obvious, there are cases where people do rush in. Always try to settle before launching court action. It will assist in the case if it does go to court.

Which court deals with a small claim

The court action can be started in any court, but the case can be transferred. If the claim is defended and the claim is for a fixed amount, the court will automatically transfer the case to a defendant's local court (if he or she is an individual not a company). In other cases, either party can ask for the case to be transferred.

Commencing a claim

The claimant commences a claim by filling in a claim form, obtainable from local county courts or legal stationers. They can also be obtained from the internet. The government court site is www.justice.gov.uk.

All forms can be obtained from this website as can a host of information on all legal topics. The form is quite straightforward and asks for details of claimant and defendant and how much is owed. The form also asks for the particulars of the claim. The particulars set out full details of the claim. If there is not enough room on the form then a separate piece of paper can be used. The claimant has a right to spend a little more time on the particulars and can send them to the defendant separately, but no later than 14 days after the claim form.

The forms are designed to be user friendly and are accompanied by guidance notes to ensure that no mistakes are made.

The claimant may be entitled to claim interest on the claim and, if so, must give details of the interest claimed in the particulars of claim. In a personal injury claim the particulars of claim must include the claimant's date of birth and brief details of the injuries. The claimant must attach a list of any past expenses and losses that they want to claim for and any expenses and losses that they may incur in the future.

Applying for the claim form to be issued

The claimant must ensure that two copies of the claim form reach the court where court action is to commence and a copy should be kept for records. There will be a fee to pay. Currently this depends on the amount of money to be claimed. You should check with your local county court, small claims division, for the current fees.

In some cases, the fee will be waived, for example if the claimant is receiving income support, working families tax credit, disabled persons tax credit or income based job seekers allowance. If none of these benefits are received, but financial hardship would be suffered if a fee was paid, the fee may also be waived. The court will stamp the claim form and then, in most cases, serve it on the defendant. The court will give the claimant a notice of issue.

Usually the court will serve the claim form by sending it to the defendant by first class post. The claimant will be deemed to have received it on the second day of posting. If the claimant wishes to serve the claim form his or herself then a request should be made and the court will provide the form and other forms that go with it.

If the case is not defended

If the defendant is not defending the case, then he or she may accept that they owe the money. If this is the case then he or she can pay the money directly to the claimant. If the defendant has accepted that they owe the money, but needs time to pay, they can propose an arrangement, for example that the amount owed is paid in instalments or all the money in one lump sum on a specified future date. If the claimant accepts this offer, he or she will have to return a form to the court requesting 'judgement by admission'. If the defendant does not keep to this agreement the claimant can then take enforcement action.

If the claimant does not accept this offer then he or she must give good reason and a court official will decide what a reasonable arrangement will be. The court will send both parties an order for payment. If the claimant is not happy with the order then he or she will have to write to the court giving reasons and sending a copy to the defendant. A judge will then decide what is reasonable for the defendant to pay. If the defendant does not keep to the arrangement, the claimant can take enforcement action.

If the defendant is defending the case

If the case is to be defended, the defendant has to respond to the claim within 14 days of service (this is the second day of posting). If the particulars of claim were served after the claim form the defendant must respond within 14 days of service of particulars of claim. A defence is launched by the defendant sending back the defence form, which was sent with the claim form.

If the defendant does not send a defence back within the time period then the claimant can ask for an order to be made against him or her. The defendant can send the defence back to the court or can send the acknowledgement of service form sent with the defence form back to court and the defence form back within 14 days of this. This helps if more time is needed. When the defence is sent to the court the court will send an allocation questionnaire to both the claimant and the defendant. This must be returned to the court no later than the date specified in it.

When the claimant returns the allocation form a fee should also be sent although this can be waived on financial grounds. The court will use the information contained within the allocation questionnaire to decide which track to allocate the case to.

When the court has decided to allocate the case to the small claims track, the claimant and defendant will be sent a notice of allocation. This form will tell the parties what they have to do to prepare for the hearing. These instructions are called 'directions'. One example of directions may be that parties are told that they should send all copies of relevant documents to court, documents that they intend to use in court in the case against the other party. These are sent at least 14 days before the case begins. There are standard directions for a number of common cases, for example, if the claim is to do with a holiday then there will be standard directions from the courts as to the evidence needed.

The day of the hearing

The notice of allocation will usually specify the time, day and date of hearing, where the hearing will take place and how much time has been allowed for it. If the claimant wants to attend the hearing but for some reason cannot, then a letter should be sent to the court requesting a different hearing date. A fee is payable and the court will only agree to this request if it is based on reasonable grounds.

A claimant can also ask the court to deal with a claim in his or her absence. A typical case might be where the costs and time to reach the court are disproportionate. If this is the case then a letter should reach the court at least seven days before the case.

In some cases, the court will not set a final hearing date. The following are alternatives used by the courts:

- The court could propose that the case is dealt with without a hearing. If both parties have no objections then the case can be decided on the papers only. If the parties do not reply by the date given then the court will usually take that silence as consent
- The court may hold a preliminary hearing. This could happen if the claim requires special directions which the judge wants to explain to the parties personally or where the judge feels that the claimant or defendant has no real prospect of succeeding and wants to sort out the claim as soon as possible to save everyone time and expense, or if the papers

do not show any reasonable grounds for bringing the claim. A preliminary hearing could become a final hearing where the case is decided.

Preparing a case

It is important that a case is prepared carefully – the court has to be convinced. A reasonable amount of time should be spent ensuring that all the facts are entered, all dates specified and all paperwork is available. The following points are a general guide to what preparation should be made:

- someone with low income can use the legal help scheme to cover the costs of legal advice, but not representation from a solicitor. This advice can be extremely useful and can include getting expert reports, for example on faulty goods. However, a report can only be used in court with permission of the court
- notes about the case should be set out in date order. This will help you to present your case and will make sense to a judge. All backing documentation should be taken to court and be presented if asked for. This documentation should be organised around the presentation, in chronological order
- damaged or faulty goods should be taken as evidence. If it is not possible to do this then photographs should be taken instead
- evidence of expenses should be taken along and any receipts kept
- all letters about the case should be taken to court
- in most cases, the claimant and defendant may be the only witnesses. If the court has agreed that other witnesses can

attend, then they must attend. If a witness has difficulty getting time off work then a witness summons can be served. The courts will explain how to do this.

The final hearing

The final hearing is usually held in public but can be held in private if the parties agree or the judge thinks that it is necessary. Hearings in the small claims track are informal and the usual rules of evidence do not apply. The judge can adopt any method of dealing with the hearing that he or she thinks fit and can also ask questions of the witnesses before anyone else. A lay representative has the right to speak on behalf of a person at a hearing but only if that party attends the hearing. If an interpreter is needed, because English is not the first language then an experienced advisor should be consulted, or the court may be able to advise on this.

At the end of the hearing the judge will pass judgement. The judge has to give reasons for the decision that he or she has arrived at. If the claimant wins, he or she will get the court fee back as well as the sum awarded. If the claimant loses no fees will be returned. However, it is unlikely that any other costs will have to be paid.

Appealing against a decision

A party may appeal against a judgement in the small claims track only if the court made a mistake in law or there was a serious irregularity in the proceedings. If a person wishes to appeal then a notice of appeal must be filed within 14 days. A fee is payable although this can be waived in cases of financial hardship. If you do wish to appeal a decision, it is very likely that you would need to consult a solicitor or an experienced advisor to help you.

Enforcement of orders

If a defendant does not pay, the claimant can go back to court and enforce that order. As we have seen, there are a number of remedies, such as bailiff, attachment of earnings and garnishee order.

****

Chapter16

Consumer Issues Generally

Buying goods in the European Union
Currently consumers in the UK and the other EU member states buying goods and services from other EU countries can rely on consumer law and safety standards which are the same or similar in every EU member state. EU consumer law creates a minimum standard for consumer law and safety standards which every EU member state must meet. Some EU member states, such as the UK with the Consumer Rights Act 2015, even choose to give consumers rights and protections which are better than the minimum standard required by EU law. In addition to harmonised consumer rights, EU consumer protection legislation also gives UK consumers the right to enforce their consumer rights in the EU and vice versa.

Divergence:
Post-Brexit, there may be a divergence between UK consumer law and consumer law in the remaining EU member states, starting on Exit Day, and potentially becoming more pronounced as time passes, even though the UK Government intends to retain some EU consumer law which is in force before Exit Day as domestic law.

The UK Government is advising that, post-Brexit, consumers will need to check the terms of consumer protection offered by the seller and the member state the seller is located in to confirm if the level of protection is different from the UK level of protection. This divergence will not only affect consumers, as businesses that trade cross-border will also have to think about having terms and conditions which comply with UK law as well as terms and conditions which are suitable for trading in the EU.

Enforcement:

Post-Brexit, making cross-border consumer purchases (e.g. online) may be less predictable for UK consumers purchasing goods and services from the EU, and vice versa, as UK and EU consumer law diverges and enforcing consumer rights cross-border becomes more difficult.

At the moment, the UK consumer protection regime is supported by a reciprocal cross-border consumer enforcement framework which allows cooperation between EU member state consumer enforcement authorities and gives consumers access to redress, in their home courts, when their rights have been breached. This will change after Exit Day if there is a no-deal Brexit.

A fundamental reduction of UK consumers' rights will also result from the fact that UK consumers will no longer be able to use the UK courts to effectively seek redress from EU based traders. Even if a UK court does make a judgment, the enforcement of that judgment will be more difficult as the UK will no longer be part of the EU. Consumers in the rest of the EU will also lose some of their rights as they will no longer be able to enforce their consumer rights against UK traders though their own home courts.

Post-Brexit, UK consumers and UK traders will also have less access to Alternative Dispute Resolution to settle disputes with traders as they will not be able to use the EU-wide Online Dispute Resolution platform which is run by the European Commission for the EU member states.

The future of UK consumer law and consumer rights

While the UK Government remains intent on finalising and approving a deal before Exit Day, it is clear that Brexit (whether negotiated or no-deal) will have a significant impact on UK consumer law and UK consumer rights, particularly where a consumer wants to enforce its consumer rights against a trader based in one of the remaining EU member states. Although the UK Government's aim is to ensure that, after Exit Day, UK consumers will retain the protections they currently have when buying from UK businesses, the UK will no longer be an EU member state, so there will be an impact on the extent to which UK consumers are protected when buying goods and services from the remaining EU member states.

Currently and until things become clearer

When buying goods or purchasing services in a member country of the European Union (The EU) your rights will be based on the law existing in that particular country. The fact that EU law is continuously pushing for harmonisation means that rights will be similar in member countries. You will have UK statutory rights and also the rights of the country where the goods were purchased if:

- you signed a contract for goods or services with a seller based in another EU country but the seller advertised in the UK and you concluded the contract in the UK. One example is you purchased clothes mail order from a company based in Spain, having seen the advert in a UK magazine and ordered from the UK;
- the seller received your order while in the UK; or
- you bought the goods and services in another UE member state during an excursion organised by the seller to encourage you to buy goods or services. You will not usually be entitled to UK statutory rights as well as those of the country of purchase if the contract involves:
- a service is provided which is not usually provided in the UK transport-there are some exceptions to this, including package travel contracts Insurance
- Land or property-although timeshare has its own specific rules (see below)

If you buy something from the internet and the seller is based in another EU member state then in most cases you will have the same statutory rights as if you had bought it from a seller based in the UK. There is a voluntary membership scheme for traders throughout the UK who use websites to sell goods or services. In the main, you will not have to pay more VAT or tax when you buy goods or services in another EU country. However, special rules apply in relation to certain goods such as nearly new cars, motorbikes and boats. More advice can be obtained from HM Revenue and Customs about these goods.

Faulty goods

The law in each EU country will determine whether or not you can return faulty goods or right faulty services, repair them or get your money back. Guarantees too will be affected by the law in the country of purchase If a problem arises.

The response to discovering that a good or service is faulty is the same as that in England: stop using the goods; find proof of purchase; if the goods in question are dangerous phone Citizens Advice Consumer Line on 03454 04 05 06; contact the seller. You could write to the seller, alternatively you could use the European Consumer Complaint Form. You can obtain a copy of this from the internet by going to the address: Asserting Consumer Rights Section at http://europa.eu/geninfo and then searching for the consumer complaint form.

If you are not satisfied with the response from the supplier then you should determine whether or not the company/person is a member of an organisation that offers conciliation or mediation. If you paid for the goods on credit, e.g. a credit card, then it may be simpler to make a claim against the credit company rather than the seller. The goods would usually have cost over £100 and under £30,000. If you are going nowhere with your complaint, and feel that there was a problem with the advertising, then you can try the

Advertising Standards Authority, which is a member of the European Standards Alliance. Refer to useful addresses at the back of the book.

If the trader does not agree with your complaint and is not part of a scheme that offers a dispute resolution service, there are other organisations which may be able to help you.

European Consumer Centres
There is a network of European Consumer Centres (ECC's) in many of the EU countries which provide information about consumer law and the procedures for enforcing your rights.

Financial Services Network (FIN-NET)
If your complaint involves financial services, the Europe-wide Financial Services Network (FIN-NET) helps resolve consumer disputes in the areas of banking, building societies, insurance and investment.

The UK member of FIN-NET is The Financial Ombudsman. They will help you by putting you into contact with a dispute resolution scheme in the country where you bought the financial service. Website: www.finacial-ombudsman.org.uk Tel: 0300 123 9 123. However, check the UK's ongoing membership after 2020.

Buying from an overseas seller outside Europe
When you buy from a trader in a country outside Europe, it may be difficult to find out what your consumer rights are. Your rights will depend on the country you bought from.

If you buy goods or services from a trader based outside the European Union (EU) your rights will depend on:

- your contract with the trader
- the laws of the country where the trader is based.

Check your terms and conditions or contract
When you bought the goods or services you may have been given a contract or terms and conditions. The terms and condition may be printed on a receipt or an order confirmation. They should contain information about some of the rights you may have, such as cancellation or delivery rights. They may also tell you what to do if you have a complaint.

The country's laws
To find out about the consumer laws in a particular country, search online for the country's trading standards or consumer rights association or visit the country's government website.

What to do if goods are faulty or the service unsatisfactory
If you have a problem with goods or services you ordered, start by making a complaint to the trader, by phone or in writing.

If you paid by credit or with a debit card
If you paid for the goods on credit or with a debit card, you might find it easier to make a claim against the credit or debit company instead of the trader. The goods must usually have cost more than

£100 and not more than £30,000 for a single item. You don't need to have put the full purchase price on your card.

Contact a consumer complaints organisation in that country
If your complaint to the trader has not been successful, you could try contacting a consumer complaints organisation in that country. Search online for the country's trading standards or consumer rights association or visit the country's government website. The following government agencies deal with customer rights and complaints in their country:

- **Australia:** Australian Competition and Consumer Commission
- **Canada** : Office of Consumer Affairs in Canada
- **New Zealand**: Ministry of Consumer Affairs in New Zealand
- **South Africa**: Provincial Consumer Affairs Offices in South Africa.

The Better Business Bureau can help with complaints about goods or services that you've bought from a trader based in the United States. You can also report a US trader to the Federal Trade Commission (FTC). The FTC may take action against the trader, but it won't sort out your individual complaint.

Use alternative dispute resolution
If your complaint to the trader has not been successful and you have been unable to get advice or help from a consumer

organisation in that country, you could get an independent person to look at your consumer problem and try and find a solution.

This is called Alternative Dispute Resolution (ADR). Search the international directory of ADR organisations for the countries listed at www.econsumer.gov

Seeking legal advice

As a last resort, If your complaint to the trader has not been successful and you have been unable to get advice or help from a consumer organisation in that country, you could seek specialised legal advice from a solicitor. However, taking up a cross-border legal action could be very stressful and expensive. You will have to decide whether it is worth it.

Recording your complaint on the international consumer complaint database

If your complaint is about something you bought online from a trader based in one of the participating countries, you may want to record it on the international consumer complaint database

Timeshare property

As most people know who have been pursued through the streets by agents, buying a timeshare buys you the right to use holiday accommodation for a set amount of time each year, i.e. one week or two weeks at a select resort or resorts. To be protected by timeshare laws, the agreement must be for at least three years.

What is described below relates to timeshares purchased from companies and not private individuals.

When you buy a timeshare, it is important to remember that you are signing a binding agreement with a timeshare company. It is difficult to cancel the agreement so it is important to get as much information before you sign, including:

- full costs, including all charges
- length of agreement-if you are signing a contract for less than three years this is usually a deliberate attempt to avoid the law
- what the area and particular resort is like
- what you legal interest is in the property and terms and conditions of the agreement
- whether there is an owners committee or association and the extent of their powers

Complaining if things go wrong

A criminal offence may have been committed if you buy a timeshare in an EEA country (see below) and:

- you ask for a brochure and this is not provided; or
- the seller takes money off you during the cooling off period (see below); or
- the seller makes false or misleading claims about the timeshare.

If you have a problem and the above applies then contact Citizens Advice Consumer line on 03454 04 05 06. Contact www.citizensadvice.org.uk for Northern Ireland or Scottish advice lines.

Cancelling a timeshare agreement

As with other consumer transaction, once you have signed a timeshare agreement, the law gives you a cooling off period during which time you can cancel the agreement and have your money back without having to pay a cancellation fee. You are entitled to a cooling off period only if the timeshare agreement is more than three years and is for a property or caravan in the EU area. This does not apply to timeshares bought before 1st May 2004 in countries which joined the EU before this date, i.e. Malta. However, check your rights once Britain departs the EU, particularly if the UK departs without a deal.

The length of the cooling off period depends on the country that you were in when the agreement was signed. If you signed the agreement in the UK the cooling off period is 14 days. In a Member Country of the European Economic Area (EEA) the cooling off period is ten days. In some EEA countries it will be necessary for a lawyer to witness the agreement. This is non-refundable if you cancel the agreement. In general, the EEA consists of EU Member states, although this should be checked with the EU website.

Timeshare companies in the UK and EEA must tell you about the cooling off period when you sign the agreement. If they don't then it will usually be extended by three months.

If there are problems with your timeshare, and thankfully over the last decade a lot of the rogues have disappeared, then your rights will very much depend on what agreement you have signed. You may need the help of a specialist lawyer to decide what law applies. The Timeshare Association can provide help and assistance. They can be contacted on 01253 208 487 or:

www.thetimeshareassociation.co.uk.

Problems with trains

National Rail Conditions of Carriage. These are the minimum levels of compensation train companies have to offer. Many offer more generous compensation than this for delays, so it's worth checking the company's site for full details.

The National Rail Conditions of Carriage are the underlying rules for train travel in Britain. These conditions set out the amount of compensation you're entitled to. The minimum compensation for a delay is 50% of your single ticket (25% of a return, unless you were delayed on both legs) if you're more than one hour late. These conditions are stingier than most of the train companies' own rules on compensation for delay.

How do I claim compensation?

The amount of compensation you're entitled to will depend on the length of your delay. Most train operators are signed up to the Delay Repay scheme. This means you can claim 50% of your journey cost if you're delayed by half an hour, regardless of the reason for the delay. If you're delayed by an hour, you'll get a refund of the full journey cost.

National Rail compensation

The National Rail Conditions of Carriage state that compensation must be provided as cash or National Rail vouchers. Having a bad experience with train travel is likely to make you less keen on going back for more so vouchers may not appeal. Importantly, if you don't want rail vouchers, you must explicitly request a cash refund or your train company may give you vouchers instead.

Season tickets and compensation

Refunds for season ticket holders tend to be calculated using the proportional daily cost of the price of your annual ticket.

Consumer Rights Act travel amendments

If you're paying to travel by train you're purchasing a service, and it must be provided with reasonable care and skill. If the service you've received falls way below the standard you'd expect, you might be entitled to claim a full or partial refund. You can also claim for consequential losses.

Train companies' duty of care-If circumstances within the control of a train company leave you stranded, any train company that can help should. It should get you to your destination or give you overnight accommodation.

Tube delays

Transport for London (TFL) offers refunds if a passenger's journey is delayed for more than 15 minutes. For tube passengers, this amounts to the fare for the single journey you were making, whether you have a season ticket or have purchased a single fare.

London Overground and TFL users have to be delayed by more than 30 minutes. You must claim within 14 days to be eligible for a refund.

Exceptions to compensation rules

Compensation often doesn't apply if delays, cancellations or poor service happened for reasons outside the train company's control, for example:

- Acts or threats of vandalism or terrorism
- Suicides or accidents involving trespassers
- Gas leaks or fires in lineside buildings not caused by a train company
- Line closures at the request of the police or emergency services
- Exceptionally severe weather conditions
- Industrial action
- Riots or civil commotion
- Fire, mechanical or electrical failure or a defect (except where caused by a train company or its trains' defects)

Compensation during engineering work

In most cases any disruption due to engineering work is heavily publicised beforehand, and most train companies will publish a revised timetable that sets out when reduced services (if any) will be running. To claim train delay compensation during engineering work you'll need to be delayed long enough to qualify under that train companies rules based on the revised timetable your train company has published, not the regular timetable.

This is not necessarily the case where engineering work overruns beyond the revised timetable. In this case you may be able to claim compensation based on the regular timetable, as long as your train company is signed up to Delay Repay.

Consumer Rights Act travel amendments
From 1st October 2016 you can claim compensation for certain types of poor service on almost all transport services, including mainline passenger rail services, coaches and ferry journeys.

Supplying a travel service
When you pay to travel by train, coach or ferry you're considered to have purchased a service. The Consumer Rights Act provides obligations on those providing the service. The provider must perform the service with reasonable care and skill. Information which is said or written is binding if you've relied on it. If the price is not agreed beforehand, the service must be provided for a reasonable price.

Unless a particular timescale for performing the service is set out or agreed, the service must be carried out in a reasonable time. Depending on how severe the failing is, you can claim back up to 100% of the price you paid.

What can I claim for?

If you're paying to travel by train, coach or ferry you're purchasing a service, and it must be provided with reasonable care and skill. In practice this could mean that you can claim a full or partial refund for things like delays, where these are caused by something the service provider has done.

You can claim a refund of up to 100% of the price paid. But, for example if a delay was short, or short in relation to the overall journey time, you may only be able to claim a partial refund.

If you claim a refund under the Consumer Rights Act it may mean you can't receive compensation from other schemes, as there's generally a rule that you can't be compensated twice for the same thing. But you're still free to start both claims.

What is a poor travel service?

If you feel the service you've received falls way below the standard you'd expect, you might be entitled to claim a full or partial refund in the following circumstances:

- A severely overcrowded train because too few carriages are available
- A service that's delayed for less than the time limit that applies under other compensation schemes
- Unavailability of a particular seat, where you've paid for a specified seat or a seat in a certain coach or carriage (such as first class)
- A consistently late running service if you have bought a season ticket

- Failure to provide access to a toilet on longer journeys
- Failure to provide food on a train journey if it was part of the described service
- The Wi-Fi service you paid for does not work

You'll need evidence to prove your claim, and be prepared to argue your case.

Claiming for consequential loss

Under the Consumer Rights Act you can claim for consequential losses. This means you can claim for financial losses you have suffered as a result of the failure by the transport service. To make a successful claim you'll need to demonstrate how your losses are linked to a breach of contract by the service provider. Your first port of call should be to write to the company asking for compensation. You should explain how their service was in breach of their contract with you and how that breach resulted in further losses to you. For example, due to a delay or cancellation you may have missed a connecting journey and had to pay for an alternative service. It's a good idea to seek out legal advice if your claim is particularly high value or complicated.

Payment protection insurance (PPI)

Everyone has witnessed the trouble that banks have experienced as a result of miss selling of PPI. Huge amounts of compensation have been paid out. It is very important to understand what PPI is, do you want it and the benefits and when to buy.

Payment protection insurance (PPI) covers loan or debt repayments if you are unable to meet them in certain situations, such as being made redundant or not being able to work because of an accident or illness.

You may have been offered or sold a PPI policy at the same time as you took out a loan, mortgage, credit card, store card, car finance or other credit. However, from 6 April 2012 a firm generally cannot sell PPI at the same time as you take out credit.

You do not have to buy PPI from the same firm and it usually pays to shop around for a deal that is right for you.

This type of cover may also be called loan protection, credit insurance, loan repayment insurance, ASU (accident, sickness and unemployment) insurance, account cover or payment cover.

How PPI covers you
The benefits of PPI and how the policy works vary depending on the terms and conditions. It will generally cover monthly loan or mortgage repayments, or at least some of them, for a set period of time. This will usually be for up to 12 months but some policies can cover your repayments for a longer period.

With credit and store cards, PPI may pay a percentage of your outstanding balance or the minimum payment each month for up to a year. This might only be for the amount you owe when you make a claim, and not any balance you build up after this.

Once the claim period has ended you will have to make any outstanding repayments yourself.

If the policy includes life insurance it will generally pay off the balance of the loan or debt if you die.

Before you buy PPI

As PPI policies can differ greatly you should shop around to find one that includes the features you need.

You should always read the key policy information before you buy. This sets out information like how long the cover lasts, the main features and benefits of the policy, and any significant or unusual exclusions or conditions.

Some PPI policy features to consider include:

- the price of the policy;
- whether you have other insurance which could cover your repayments;
- any limits on the amount of benefit you may receive from a claim on the policy;
- the period of time the policy will cover your loan or debt repayments;
- whether the cover starts as soon as you make a claim or after a certain amount of time;
- the types of injuries and accidents covered, and those that may be excluded (e.g. stress or back complaints);
- whether it covers injuries or illness that you have had before taking out the policy;
- how long you have to be employed on a permanent contract before you can make a claim; and
- whether the policy covers you if you are self-employed.

PPI is not the only product that can protect you against loss of income and may not always be the right one for your circumstances. A couple of alternatives are income protection, which is not linked to a debt but covers loss of income, and short-term protection insurance.

Supplier of goods/services has gone out of business

If the supplier has gone out of business your action and the outcome will very much depend on the status of the trader, whether limited company, sole trader or partnership. If payments were made by credit card the credit card company may be liable if the amount is more than £100 and less than £30,000. This will not apply if the payment was made by debit card.

Sole trader/partnership

Sole traders or partnerships remain liable even if they have ceased to trade. You should get advice from Citizens Advice Consumer line before taking court action. It is only worth taking action if the trader is able to pay. If the trader has gone bankrupt then it is not worth pursuing the matter. You would need to join the queue of other creditors following notification of bankruptcy.

Limited company

If the supplier is a limited company, it may have gone into administration or liquidation. If the company goes into administration, an administrator will be appointed. The administrator will see if the company can be rescued or sold rather than being liquidated. A limited company can go into voluntary liquidation following a shareholders decision that the company is no longer solvent. The company can also go into liquidation following a court order. Once in liquidation, a liquidator is appointed to redistribute all the company's assets. This is known as winding up. The liquidator will send the final accounts to the Registrar of Companies and the company will be dissolved three months later. You may be able to find out the status of a company by contacting Companies House on 0303 1234 500 or the website at www.companieshouse.co.uk. For all other matters in relation to money/goods/services owed then you should contact the liquidator of the company.

Buy now pay later deals

We discussed these types of deals in the previous chapter on credit. The financial regulator has tightened rules for companies that charge customers interest on 'buy now pay later' policies in an attempt to tackle high cost credit that disproportionately affects vulnerable people. From November 2019, companies that offer these 'buy now pay later' credit, such as store cards and financing arrangements on items bought from catalogues will be banned from charging backdated interest on purchases. Buy now pay later deals usually includes a one year promotional period, during which customers do not have to make payments and are not charged interest. If the customer does not pay back the sum owed during that year, interest is charged from the date of purchase. This has now been outlawed.

Dry cleaning

Dry cleaning is an area where significant numbers of people experience problems. As with other goods/services supplied, the law underpinning this particular service states that the dry cleaning must be carried out with care, finished within a reasonable time and provided at a reasonable cost to the consumer.

On the whole, dry cleaning can only achieve a finish that is dependant on the condition of the garment in the first place. It may serve to highlight existing wear and tear of the garment that cannot be claimed for. However, if you feel that the item has been poorly cleaned then it is reasonable to ask for a refund. You should allow the company to re-clean the product of offered. Compensation may be payable if the contract was breached and the dry cleaning was not carried out in time or with care. It may also be payable if there has been negligence or any second cleaning has not solved the problem.

If you have a problem with dry cleaning you should take the item back and ask to speak to the manager or you should write a clear letter outlining the fault. Explain the problem and ask for refund, repair or compensation. Like many organisations, dry cleaning has its own umbrella organisation, the Textile Services Association (TSA). They provide a conciliation services if the dry cleaner in question is a member. They can be reached on 0203 151 5600 . If they are not a member or you do not wish to use their services, you can obtain the services of an expert witness, such as an independent test house. One such test house is the Dry Cleaning Technology Centre 01943 816545. At the end of the whole process, if the dry cleaner refuses to cooperate and you feel that you are getting nowhere then you can resort to the small claims court to solve your action. This will only be really feasible if you have tried all other avenues and you have kept all records and receipts along with the evidence.

Mobile phones

Many people experience problems with mobile phones and seek redress against the supplier. The phone, at the end of the day, is like other goods and services. The law says that it should:

- match its description
- be of satisfactory quality

These rights exist wherever you buy the phone (with the exception of purchase off a private individual.

You will not be successful in any action against a seller if you examined the phone and the fault was obvious but you went ahead and purchased the phone. Once bought, you cannot take action if you change your mind. Likewise, the usual stipulations exist concerning wear and tear.

The service from the mobile phone provider must be carried out with reasonable care and carried out in a reasonable time and delivered at a reasonable cost. The rules concerning credit cards or credit agreements apply to mobile phones as to all other goods.

If you have a problem with a handset it is the seller and not the manufacturer or service provider who is liable for rectifying the problem. If you have a problem with service then it is to the service provider that you should turn to seek redress.

If you bought the phone after 31st March 2003, you can ask the seller to repair or replace it free of charge if it is faulty. If you do this within six months of receiving the phone it will be assumed that the problem existed when you purchased it, unless the seller can demonstrate otherwise. You can still ask for a replacement or repair within six years of purchasing the phone if it is reasonable for it to have lasted that long. If it is impossible to replace or repair the phone and the fault persists then it is reasonable to ask for a full or partial refund. You may be entitled to some form of compensation if the phone is not fit for purpose, the contract with the provider has been breached, the phone is unsafe or dangerous, the seller has made a false statement or any repair undertaken or inadequate service has not rectified the problem.

There are several organisations that deal with complains against mobile phone companies. Office of the Telecommunications Ombudsman (OTELO) is chief amongst these. They can be contacted on 0330 440 1614 www.ombudsman-services.org. The Communication and Internet Services Adjudication Scheme (CISAS) may also be able to help. In common with many organisations that offer help, they will insist that you have exhausted the company's own complaints procedure first. They can be contacted on 020 7520 3814or www.cisas.org.uk.

Private sales including boot sales
When goods are purchased from a private individual, either from an advert in the paper or from a boot sale, the law lays down the basic requirement that the goods must match their description, i.e. they

must be as described by the seller. It is very important to check goods when you purchase them as the private seller is not liable for faulty goods. However, it is an offence for a private seller to sell a car that is un-roadworthy. If a business sells goods purporting to be a private seller then this is a criminal offence and you should contact Citizens Advice Consumer Line on 03454 04 05 06 immediately.

As with all other areas involving transactions between buyer and seller evidence of purchase should be kept along with all other evidence. This will be needed, as the final resort is the small claims court. Remember, it is purchases of goods or services from a private vendor which offers the least legal protection.

Buying at auction

As with most other circumstances, when goods are purchased, they must match their description and be of satisfactory quality and fit for purpose. These requirements were set out in the Sale of Goods Act 1979, now replaced by The Consumer Rights Act 2015. Your rights under this Act apply to all new goods bought at auction and also second hand goods purchased where you did not have the opportunity to attend to inspect the goods, i.e. internet auctions. If you buy at auction you may not have these rights if:

- the goods are second hand and you have the opportunity to attend the sale in person
- you are informed that the Sale of Goods Act 1979 does not apply or that goods are sold as seen and the auctioneer can demonstrate that this is reasonable.

When you purchase goods at auction you will enter into a contract with the owner of the goods, not the auctioneer. If there is a problem with the goods then you should take action against the owner of the goods not the auctioneer. The auction house is not under any obligation to give you the owner's details. If you bought new goods at an auction after 31st March 2003, or second hand goods at an auction where you cannot attend in person you can ask the trader to replace the goods free of charge or repair them if faulty. A last resort is the small claims court. However, remember that buying goods at auction can be similar to buying from a private individual and it is only worth pursuing a case if you feel confident of winning.

Remember, auctions, especially internet auctions are not the safest environments from which to purchase goods and the utmost care must be taken to ensure that money is not lost or goods are not faulty.

Banks and building societies

Banks are the same as other service providers when it comes to the provision of goods and services, they must carry out their business with reasonable care and skill, in reasonable time and at reasonable cost. This last point has been a bone of contention recently, particularly in relation to bank charges.

The Banking Code

The Banking Code sets out minimum standards of service for banks, building societies and credit card companies providing personal banking services. Although not mandatory to sign up to the code, most banks and building societies along with credit card companies do.

Banks and others signed up to the code must act fairly and in a reasonable manner in all its dealings with customers. If it breaches the code then in keeping with all other Ombudsman Services, you should first exhaust the complaints procedure of the bank or other concerned. After this has failed to rectify the matter then you can complain to the Financial Services Ombudsman (see below).

Bank charges

This is one area which has hit the headlines recently. Banks charging very high fees for unauthorised overdrawn customers. Banks and building societies are allowed to charge for their services, which must be clearly set out. Banks can charge default charges, being charges for typically exceeding your overdraft limit. The bank or building society is only allowed to charge what it costs to cover their administrative charges. This has not been the case, and if they charge you more than this you may have a legal right to be refunded the difference. If you think that your default charges are unreasonably high you should ask the bank to refund the difference. More information concerning this procedure can be found at www.which.net/campaigns.

Overdraft charges new rules from 2020

Fixed daily and monthly overdraft fees are banned and replaced with a single interest rate from April 2020. An unarranged overdraft – one you haven't agreed with your bank before you use it – will no longer be able to cost more than an arranged overdraft under the new rules, and banks won't be able to charge you just for having an overdraft.

The price of each overdraft will be a single interest rate, rather than fixed fees of a certain amount per day or month. This price must be advertised using an annual percentage rate (APR) to help consumers compare costs across different accounts. The overdraft price rules came into force on 6 April 2020.

The Financial Conduct Authority (FCA) also says banks must do more to identify customers in financial difficulty and help them reduce overdraft use, starting from this December.

If you approach a bank or building society with a complaint make sure that you have copies of all evidence (statements etc). Either speak to your account manager or write to the branch manager. If you are not satisfied with the response then you should ask for details of the complaints procedure. Find out whether the bank subscribes to the Banking Code of Practice. A copy of this code can be obtained either from the bank in question or from the British Bankers Association at www.bba.org.uk

When you have completed each stage of the internal complaints procedure of the organisation concerned you will be sent a letter of deadlock if the complaint has not been solved.

You can then use the Financial Ombudsman Service. Your complaint must be brought to the Ombudsman within six months of the deadlock letter. The Ombudsman will try to deal with your complaint informally but if this fails will make a preliminary decision. After the consumer and bank involved have made comments on this preliminary decision then the Ombudsman will make a final ruling or recommendation. If you are still not satisfied then you can take court action. the Ombudsman can be contacted on 0800 023 4567 or www.financial-ombudsman.org.uk.

Motor Insurance

If you drive a car or leave it parked on a road, then it must be insured. There are three main types of insurance:

- Third party which is the minimum amount of cover you can have. This covers you for damage to someone else's vehicle or property or injury to someone which arises as a result of an accident involving your car
- Third party fire and theft. This includes the above with the addition of theft and fire
- Comprehensive insurance. This includes the above two categories but also pays for repairs to your car and can cover you for a host of other eventualities if requested and paid for such as legal and medical, hire of another vehicle etc.

When taking out insurance it is necessary to give the insurer as much information as possible otherwise the policy could be invalidated. When you first take out insurance you will get a cover note. It is a criminal offence to drive without this cover note or a full policy note.

There may be certain circumstances where your insurance policy is found to be invalid.

These can be:

- someone who is not on your policy drives your car
- your car is found to be unroadworthy-third party claims should still be accepted
- you do not have a valid driving licence
- the insurer believes that you are partly to blame for the accident-they may only pay part of the damage
- your insurer has gone out of business and cannot meet the claim. In this case you may be able to get compensation from the Financial Services Compensation Scheme (FCS). If the insurer is a member of Lloyds contact the Lloyds Complaints Department on 020 7327 5693.

Stolen vehicle

If your car has been stolen you should inform the police and insurer immediately. The insurer will wait several weeks before settling the claim in case the car is found. If you were paying your premium by instalments you will usually need to pay the full year even if the car has been stolen. If the car is not found the insurer will usually pay the then current market value of the car, which is almost certain to be different than the price you paid for it.

Claiming if in an accident

If you have an accident you should never admit liability. This is a matter for the insurers and the police. Always exchange names and addresses and insurance details with the other driver(s). Always take the registration number. If, as sometimes happens, the other person refuses to give you details of their insurance your insurer may be able to trace the insurer via the registration number. Tell the insurer about the accident immediately. If someone has been injured or the other person is under the influence of drink or drugs call the police immediately.

If you are making a claim against the other driver write to them informing them of this. State that you hold them responsible for the accident and also send a copy of the letter to your insurer. The other driver must report the accident to their insurer before the matter can be dealt with. The insurer can only act on the instructions of their own policy holder. If you need to find out details of the other persons policy, or whether they have one you should look up the motor insurance database by contacting the Motor Insurers Bureau on www.mib.org.uk or 01908 830 001.

If the driver was uninsured or cannot be identified then the Motor Insurers Bureau may be able to settle your claim, even where the other driver is uninsured. If you have a comprehensive policy then you should claim from your own insurer. You will still need to claim from the other drivers policy for any injuries suffered as a result of the accident or any losses which are not covered directly by your own policy. One more important point to note. When claiming, always weigh the economic benefits up against the loss of your no-claims bonus.

Driving overseas

Your policy will cover you for third party to drive in a European Union Country if your insurer is EU based. Your policy may also include third party cover to drive in a non-EU country. You should check these details with your insurer. Your insurer can issue you with a green card to show that you have increased cover. It may be necessary in certain non-EU countries to show this. Check the position following BREXIT as the situation will change.

Motor cycle insurance
There are two types of insurance covering motor cycles:

- Specified cycle policy which covers you to ride a specific motor cycle
- Rider policy which will cover you to ride any motorcycle up to a specified cc with the owner's permission.

Motor cycle insurance is usually limited to one person only. If someone else wants to ride your motor bike then they must be named on your policy or have their own policy. Generally, no-claims bonuses are not available for motorcycles.

If problems arise with your car or motor cycle insurance then it will, in common with other areas of goods and services, be necessary to exhaust your insurer's complaints procedure first. All insurers must be covered by the rules of the Financial Conduct Authority. This will mean that if you have a complaint, and you cannot resolve it with your insurer, and it is a legitimate complaint then you can take it to the Financial Ombudsman Service. For more information you should telephone 0800 023 4567 or go to their website on www.financial-ombudsman.org.uk

Dealing with Builders

This is an area that represents major problems for many people. Like many other providers of goods and services, when building work is carried out then it must be carried out with reasonable care and skill, finished within a reasonable time and provided at a reasonable cost. Goods or material provided must match their description and be of satisfactory quality.

However, before you can deal effectively with a building related problem you must first have a clear understanding of who your contract is with. It could be the builder, the architect/structural engineer (depending on the type and complexity of the work), the individual contractor or the subcontractor. Once identified then action can be taken. If you cannot identify who exactly is responsible then you should join them all in the action. You should also look into any guarantees that have been offered to see if they are relevant. Reliance on a guarantee does not take away your statutory right. As with other goods and services, special rules apply if you have used a credit card to pay. If the amount spent is over £100 or under £30,000 then the credit card company may be equally liable for any breach of contract.

Cancellation of building work

If you have recently signed a credit agreement away from the traders premises (i.e. at your own home) and the contract was signed after a face to face discussion with the trader, you may have a short period within which you can cancel (cooling off period). If the contract was signed on the traders business premises you may be able to withdraw from the agreement if you notify the credit company immediately and confirm the withdrawal in a letter sent by recorded delivery.

If you are not buying by credit but have signed a contract in your own home and wish to cancel, you should check the contract for cancellation rights. See above for advice about buying on the doorstep.

Finally, do not sign any documents or pay the final instalment due until you are totally satisfied. The majority of builders are honest and trustworthy. As with all walks of life there are the inadequate companies or individuals who are not.

Rights if work or goods and materials supplied are unsatisfactory
Refunds

If you have already paid a deposit to a builder and the work has not yet commenced and the trader is in breach of contract then you should be entitled to a refund of monies owed. If work has started then it is seen as reasonable that you allow the trader to rectify the fault, unless there is a specific reason why this should not be the case, i.e. the work has been left in such a dangerous condition that you feel that another builder is appropriate.

Replacement or repair

If you buy goods from a trader who installs them for you, you can ask the trader to replace or repair the goods free of charge if they are faulty or if they were installed without reasonable care or skill.

You can ask for a refund if it is impossible to replace or repair the goods.

Compensation

You may be entitled to compensation if the work was not carried out in a reasonable time or with reasonable skill or negligence is apparent.

If you have incurred additional expenses as a result of faulty workmanship or goods then you may also be entitled to compensation. In the first instance you should contact the trader to solve the problem. Make sure all documents and other evidence have been retained.

If you cannot agree responsibility with the trader you should ascertain whether or not the trader is a member of a conciliation or mediation service. It may be necessary also to obtain an expert opinion. If the matter cannot be resolved then the last resort is the small claims court.

Organisations that deal with complaints against builders
Architects Registration Board

All architects must belong to the ARB and follow their code of conduct. They can be contacted on 020 7580 5861. www.arb.org.uk

Royal Institute of British Architects (RIBA)

Almost all architects belong to RIBA which has an internal scheme to deal with arbitration and conciliation. They can be contacted on 0207 580 5533 www.architecture.com

Federation of Master Builders. The Master Bond Scheme

The FMB gives advice on how to choose a builder and details of its members in your area. It has a complaints procedure and an independent arbitration service.

The MasterBond Scheme is part of the FMB. Builders who are members of the scheme are according to following its principles and practices. Their work is covered by a warranty scheme which is backed by an insurance company. There is an extra charge to be covered by this warranty.

In all cases, you should choose a reputable builder who is a member of such a federation. This will give you added protection. To find out about the FMB or the MasterBond scheme go to www.fmb.org.uk or 0330 333 7777.

Saving for Christmas

There are a number of ways of saving for Christmas. After the Farepak debacle, and other failures, in which many consumers lost money the need for sound advice is paramount. The following are considered safe methods of saving for Christmas, each with their own particular advantages and disadvantages outlined.

Standard bank and building society accounts

- You get interest on your money
- You sometimes get a bonus
- Your money is protected up to a limit
- Its up to you when you take your money out
- They will not collect money from your home

- They do not pay out in vouchers
- You do not have to buy from a particular shop or supplier

In short, saving with a bank or building society is perhaps the safest way of ensuring that you will keep hold of your money!

Special building society Christmas account
- You get interest on your money
- You will get a bonus
- You may lose that bonus and have to close your account if you take the money out early
- Your money is protected up to a limit if the building society goes bust
- They do not pay out in vouchers
- Most pay out before Christmas
- You do not have to buy from a particular shop or supplier

Credit Union savings account
- You may get a dividend
- Sometimes credit unions will pay you a bonus
- They will not collect money from your home
- If the credit union in England, Scotland and Wales goes bust, you money is protected up to a set limit
- They do not pay out in vouchers
- It is up to you when you pay your money out
- You do not have to buy from a particular shop or supplier

Special credit union Christmas savings account

- You may get a dividend
- Sometimes credit unions will pay you a bonus
- If you take money out early you may lose the dividend or bonus and have to close the account
- If a credit union in England, Scotland or Wales goes bust, your money is protected up to a certain point. For Northern Ireland check with the Companies Register
- Some credit unions pay out in vouchers
- They will pay out just before Christmas
- You do not have to buy from a particular shop or supplier.

Christmas clubs with local shops

- You will not get interest on your money
- They do not pay a bonus
- It could be difficult for you to take money out before the run-up to Christmas
- They will not collect the money from your home
- If the shop closes or goes bust you are not protected and, just like Farepak, you are unlikely to get all or any of your money back
- They do not pay out in vouchers
- You will have to buy from a particular shop or supplier

Hamper schemes

- You will not get interest on your money
- You will get a bonus

- They will make it difficult for you to take your money out before the run-up to Christmas
- They will collect money from your home
- If the company goes bust you are unlikely to get all your money back
- They pay out in vouchers
- They will pay out just before Christmas
- You will have to buy from a particular shop or supplier

Supermarket stamp schemes for Christmas
- You will not get interest on your money
- You will get a bonus
- They will make it difficult for you to take your money out before Christmas
- They will not collect money from your home
- If the company goes bust you are unlikely to get your money back

Supply of Gas and electricity-issues
You could save money by switching tariffs or energy suppliers but comparing suppliers and choosing the right deal can be confusing. In addition, there have been a number of new suppliers taking peoples money then going into administration so beware!

Energy suppliers can offer you up to four core tariffs for gas and four core tariffs for electricity. A tariff means the rate you pay for gas and electricity. Check which tariff suits your circumstances then compare tariffs between suppliers. Find out which services the energy supplier provides and which discounts may be available to you.

If you sign a contract with a new energy supplier you have a cancellation period of 14 days during which time you can cancel if you change your mind. The Citizens Advice consumer service can provide you with more information.

Choosing a supplier

The price charged for gas and electricity varies between energy suppliers. They can offer up to four core gas and four core electricity tariffs and contracts that give you a choice over how you manage and pay for your gas and electricity. To make it easier to understand your bill, there is only one charging structure made up of a standing charge and the unit prices of the gas and electricity. You should obtain as much information as you can on the different energy suppliers and their products before switching. Be aware that if one energy supplier cuts/increases its prices the others may follow. Wait until prices stabilise before going ahead.

It is important that you calculate how much energy you are currently using and how much you pay for it. This will ensure that any comparisons you make between tariffs, services and contracts are accurate. The method you use to pay for your gas and electricity (as in direct debit or other payment method) will also be a financial factor. You can check your online statement, your annual statement (if you still receive a paper copy) or ask your current supplier to help you work it out. You can then use this information to compare suppliers or to see if your current supplier can offer a cheaper deal.

There are price comparison websites that will help you find a better deal. Consider using price comparison websites that are signed up to the Ofgem Confidence Code. This code of practice, which is managed by Ofgem (the UK gas and electricity regulator), sets out the rules that member price comparison websites must abide by. They must be independent, impartial and the information must be accurate. For more information visit the Ofgem website

You can also receive advice and information on switching your supplier from the Citizens Advice consumer service.

Energy tariffs and discounts
Tariffs offered by energy suppliers take account of the type of meter you have (standard or prepayment).

These may include:

- standard tariff
- green tariffs - support environmental schemes
- fixed price - guarantees the unit price you pay for your energy for a specified time
- capped tariff - guarantees the unit price of your energy will not rise above a specified level for a specified time.
- feed in tariff - If you generate your own electricity, by having solar panels installed for example, you will be on a feed in tariff where you are paid by your energy supplier for the electricity you have generated.

Your energy supplier can also offer a discount for having a dual fuel account (you get your gas and electricity from the same supplier) or managing your account online.

What should I ask before signing a contract?

Before you agree to a contract and after you sign, the energy supplier is legally obliged to provide you with certain information. Ask your prospective new supplier to go through the main points of the contract before you sign.

Process of switching supplier

The transfer process can take about three weeks after your cancellation period has ended and is organised by your new supplier. You should inform your current supplier that you intend to switch. Your new supplier will contact you for your meter readings - always keep your own record of these readings. Your current supplier has the right to object to a transfer - if you are in debt with them, for example. Ask about arrangements for paying off outstanding debts.

Will I be able to change my mind once I've agreed a contract?

The Consumer Contracts (Information, Cancellation and Additional Charges) Regulation 2013 give you a right to cancel most contracts.

If you agree a contract 'off premises' such as on your doorstep, at home or at your place of work or at a 'distance' and without face-to-face contact with the supplier such as via the internet or by phone or email you may have a 14 day cancellation period.

Double charging

The process of switching suppliers does not always run smoothly. Watch out for an overlap where your old supplier continues to charge you when a new supplier has taken over your supply. If this happens, try to resolve it directly with the supplier that has incorrectly charged you. Provide details of the new supplier's contract and start date and ensure it has your final meter readings, as agreed with the new supplier.

Energy miss-selling

All energy suppliers are required to meet standards set by Ofgem that deal with how gas and electricity is sold to you. The main energy suppliers have signed up to the Energysure code of practice that sets out expected standards in doorstep selling practice.

The energy supplier or its representative may fail to meet their obligations - you may have been subjected to high pressure selling, been misled over features of a particular service, given false information on potential savings, had your contract falsified or progressed without your consent. You may only become aware of this when you receive a 'welcome' letter or copy contract from a new supplier. You have the right to complain. Please see our 'what can I do if I have a complaint?' section of this leaflet for details of who you can complain to.

If you believe you have been transferred by mistake or without your consent, you can switch back. Ofgem introduced the Erroneous Transfer Customer Charter. It recommends best practice for suppliers including writing to a consumer to verify that they do want to switch before going ahead. In the event of an erroneous transfer, you can contact either the old supplier or the new one to complain. Within five working days, you should be given clear information on the steps which will be taken to resolve the matter and, if you request it, details of compensation arrangements. Within 20 working days, you should be informed that you are being returned to your old supplier.

Some suppliers have moved away from cold call doorstep selling as a method of persuading consumers to switch, as they recognise that consumers do not like being pressured on the doorstep.

What can I do if I have a complaint?

In the first instance contact your energy supplier to give them the opportunity to resolve your complaint. Check your bill or visit the energy supplier's website for details on where to direct your complaint. You can contact Ombudsman Services: Energy. This organisation is approved by Ofgem to deal with consumer complaints about energy bills, misselling, problems with energy supply, Green Deal and problems with switching supplier. The service is independent and free for consumers.

- You can contact the Citizens Advice consumer service for advice and guidance on switching supplier as well as seeking advice on a complaint.

- **Gas and electricity competition - consumer checklist**
- Beware of bogus callers - always ask for and check identification.

- Never be pressured into signing a contract. If you have doubts - **do not sign**.
- If you are asked to sign any document, such as an introduction form or proof of visit form, check that it is not an agreement. If you have any doubts - **do not sign**.
- If you have any special requirements such as a pre-payment meter or arrangements for paying bills, check that the supplier can accommodate you. The supplier is not allowed to refuse your business on the basis that you have special requirements.
- How much will the gas or electricity cost? If you are looking at price comparison tables check that the same level of service is on offer.
- Is the contract rolling or a fixed time contract? Rolling contracts last for as long as you want them to.
- How long is the contract? Will you be tied to that supplier for a number of years? What about cancellation charges?
- Are there any standing charges? If so, how much?
- What payment options are there?
- How often will you get a bill or statement?
- What other services are on offer? Are there any energy saving measures that could reduce the bill?
- Check what the switching arrangements are if you have a smart meter
- Are there any dual fuel deals that could reduce the bill?
- What help can the supplier give to repair or service your boiler, gas or electricity appliances?

- What help can the supplier offer if you have difficulty paying your bills?
- Give your existing supplier 28 days notice of your intention to switch.
- Take a meter reading on the determined date of transfer to ensure that you are not charged twice for the same fuel.

Sales representatives can be **very** persuasive so be careful. Don't commit yourself until you are totally satisfied that you have all the information you need and **never** sign a document until you have read the small print.

Coronavirus scams 2021

Scams are among the most prevalent types of crime in the UK, and coronavirus is creating a perfect environment for fraudsters to thrive using a range of loathsome tactics. On Friday 20 March, City of London Police reported a 400% increase in scams as a result of coronavirus-related fraud. 105 reports had also been sent to Action Fraud, the UK's national reporting centre for fraud and cybercrime, with total losses reaching nearly £970,000. These scams range from emails that come with a nasty payload of malware and those sending you to phishing sites, to reports of criminals knocking on front doors offering to go shopping for people who are self-isolating at home. Others are related to online shopping scams involving sought-after items like face masks and hand sanitizer, and fake websites include imitating HMRC to offer tax relief.

Dealing with online scams-Ten ways to thwart the online fraudsters

We are all becoming more vulnerable to financial scammers, but there are simple steps you can take to outwit them. Fraudsters are getting more sophisticated and scams are on the rise. With 3.9 million cases reported last year, you are much more likely to experience fraud than a violent crime. Here are the best ways to avoid falling victim.

1 Choose a theme and stick to it

We all have to remember dozens of passwords these days so it is tempting to make them very simple. The best way to avoid accounts being hacked, though, is to choose long combinations of numbers, symbols and letters. To make them easier to remember, opt for a theme rather than just a memorable bit of information about you. For example, if you like Christmas, you could make it Chr*stm@$63. You can use favourite poems, songs or films. The options are endless.

2 Lie about personal information

When it comes to security questions for online accounts, you don't have to answer truthfully. Avoid giving your mother's maiden name because this is usually easy to find in electoral records or on your Facebook account. And unless you have shown remarkable restraint on social media, your pet's name is also likely to have ended up online, so don't use that either. Your answer can be anything. It could be Pick a random but memorable words, keep it secret and use it for every answer.

3 Set up extra security, but not by text

Passwords are a weak form of security, but you can add an extra layer by turning on two-step authentication for your online accounts. This means that you will receive a code that must then be produced to prove your identity when you make an online transaction. Try to avoid receiving the codes by text because they can be intercepted by fraudsters who convince your phone company to give them control of your number. Facebook. Twitter and Google give you the choice of receiving the code in an authenticator application over the internet. Ask your bank if you can receive the codes in your mobile banking application (if you use one), or by card reader; email or phone call.

4 Hang up on strangers, even your bank

Fraudsters can use software that can make it seem as though they are calling or texting you from your bank's number. If your bank tries to call you, insist on calling back using the number on the back of your debit card and from a different phone line , if possible. Be suspicious about calls from people you do not know, particularly if you are being asked for private information, bank details or any mobile-switching code that was texted to you from a phone company. Don't be afraid to hang up and call your bank to check whether it would ask you for these details. A legitimate company will understand.

5 Don't click on email links

Apply the same suspicion to any link sent to you by someone you do not know, whether by text or by email. If HM Revenue & Customs, Amazon, Apple, a parcel service or any other company suddenly emails when you are not expecting it, be suspicious and don't reply. Clicking on links can allow malicious software to be downloaded on to your phone or computer. They can also lead you to fraudulent websites that send your details to criminals. Check that the https at the start of the web address does contain the "s", which stands for secure and shows that the website is genuine.

6 Use a fine-tooth comb

Don't ignore bank statements. Scan them in detail for any strange payments. This is the best way of acting fast if you have fallen victim to fraud. Challenger banks such as Monzo will send you immediate notifications when you make a payment. If your bank does not offer this, print off your statement and highlight anything you do not recognise. If a payment description on your statement is an incomprehensible string of letters, type it into Google to find out which company uses this code.

7 Spy on your children

It sounds sneaky, but it is vital to keep a watchful eye on the social media accounts of your children. Ideally, only let your children use social media if they let you follow their profiles. This means that you can make sure they are not posting any personal information about the family online. Bank details are not the only risk, teach them not to post the dates on which you are going on holiday, pet names, or dats of birth of family members.

Also help them to understand the false lure of "easy money", a catch-phrase often used in social media posts seeking to draw young people into money-laundering activities.

8 Get proof of delivery

If you are selling used items on eBay and send them by post, make sure you ask the courier for proof of delivery. It is more expensive, but otherwise the person receiving your item can claim that they never received it and will be able to dispute the transaction and get a refund from Paypal, the payment platform. If you hand over the goods in person and therefore can't get proof of delivery, ask to be paid in cash.

9 Be careful with payments

It has become so easy to send money online that we have all become a little blasé' about it. Fraudsters prey on this. A common tactic is to hack into the emails of building contractors, plumbers or estate agents, supplying fake bank details. If you receive one of these emails, check directly with the company and be wary if it says that its payment details have suddenly changed. Dating fraud is also on the rise, with 4,555 so-called romance scams reported to the official crime reporting organisation Action Fraud last year.

Be wary of increasingly sophisticated deception techniques. For example, fraudsters can use footage of people that they have never met to make you think that you are speaking to a real person in a video call online and to convince you that they are in need of money.

10 Take five

If you only remember one thing, it should be that nothing is as urgent as it seems. Only criminals or stressed relatives will try to panic you into making payments or handing over information in a great hurry. Investments, shopping deals and online forms can wait five minutes. Take a deep breath and ring your bank or a friend to check that what you are being asked is legitimate.

****

Chapter 17

Consumer Law in Scotland

As discussed in the introduction to this book, many of the consumer laws referred to in this book apply to Scotland as well as the rest of the United Kingdom. The Consumer Rights Act 2015 applies in Scotland as well as England and Wales. However, there are some differences, notably in the use of the court system to obtain remedies.

Scottish law gives consumers five years, as opposed to six, after a purchase to take action if a problem has been discovered.

Consumers in Scotland and those who have bought items in Scotland have significantly different legal rights in the Scottish court system. For civil disputes, people take action mainly in the Sheriff Courts. Most consumer disputes are heard under a special small claims part of the 'summary cause' proceedings which, like the small claims procedure in the English, Welsh and Northern Irish county courts, is designed to be used without the need for solicitors. It has a maximum limit of £750. It is also possible to bring an action under a normal (and more formal) 'summary cause' proceedings up to a maximum of £1500. Above this limit, consumers have to use the 'ordinary cause' proceedings in the Sheriff Court, or, if they choose, the Outer House of the Court Session. Court proceedings in the Scottish Courts do differ considerably from the rest of the United

Kingdom. Trading Standards Departments in Scotland enforce criminal consumer laws in the same way as the rest of the UK. They do not prosecute offenders themselves but investigate the facts and submit reports to the Procurator Fiscal where necessary. It is the Procurator Fiscal who decides whether or not prosecution is in the public interest. Claims for compensation for aggrieved consumers can be submitted by the Trading Standards Department in their report to the procurator Fiscal.

Scottish Criminal Law requires that most evidence is corroborated i.e. evidence is provided from two independent sources.

This is a very brief overview of the main differences between Scottish law and the rest of the UK. Separate publications deal with Scottish Consumer law in more depth.

****

Appendix 1

SAMPLE LETTERS OF COMPLAINT

For a detailed, up=to-date sample of letters concerning all aspects of consumer problems go to www.citizensadvice.org.uk/consumer/template-letters.

The following are the letters listed.
Faulty goods
Letter to complain about faulty goods bought from a company
Letter to complain about misdescribed goods bought from a private seller
Letter to complain about faulty goods bought on hire purchase
Letter to complain about faulty goods supplied with a service
Letter to warn trader about court action for faulty goods
Problems with services or traders
Letter to complain to a trader about poor quality work
Letter to complain about the poor standard of a service
Letter to complain about a delay to a service
Letter to complain about a phone, TV or internet bill
Letter to 'make time of the essence': services
Letter to claim damages for misrepresented goods or services
Letter to cancel a contract that's been breached
Letter to complain to a phone company about cashback
Letter to end contract due to poor work and 'lost faith'

Problems with delivery

Letter to say you received goods or services you didn't ask for

Letter to 'make time of the essence': goods

Letter to complain about non-delivery of goods You've changed your mind

Letter to cancel a service arranged online, over the phone or by mail order

Letter to cancel or return goods bought online, over the phone or by mail order

Letter to cancel goods or services bought at home or in a public place

Holidays

Letter to complain about a holiday

Letter to ask for a refund or alternative when a package holiday is changed

Credit agreements and creditors

Letter to cancel a credit agreement before it starts

Letter to get a loan fee refunded when the loan hasn't arrived

Letter to ask to be placed on list of unsecured creditors

Letter to make a claim for equal liability from a credit provider

Energy

Letter to complain to an energy supplier

Letter to complain about energy back-billing

Letter to complain about energy mis-selling

Letter to complain about your energy supply being switched without your agreement

Useful Addresses

Advertising Standards Authority
Mid City Place
71 High Holborn
London
WC1V 6QT
Tel: 020 7492 2222
Fax: 020 7242 3696
http://www.asa.org.uk

Association of British Travel Agents (ABTA)
ABTA Ltd
30 Park Street
London
SE1 9EQ
0191 2015050
www.abta.com

Association of Independent Tour Operators (AITO)
18 Bridle Lane
Twickenham
Middlesex
TW1 3EG
020 8744 9280
http://www.aito.co.uk/

Association of Manufacturers of Domestic Electrical Appliances

Rapier House
40-46 Lamb's Conduit Street
London
WC1N 3NW
Tel: 020 7405 0666
www.thenbs.com
Email: info@amdea.org.uk|

Association of British Insurers

One America Square
17 Crosswall
London
EC3N 2LB
www.abi.org.uk
020 7600 3333

British Standards Institution

389 Chiswick High Road
London
W4 4AL
United Kingdom
0345 080 9000
http://www.bsigroup.co.uk/en/

Consumers Association (Which?)

Which?

2 Marylebone Road

London

NW1 4DF

020 7770 7000

http://www.which.co.uk

Citizens Advice Consumer Service (Formerly Consumer Direct)

03454 04 05 06

www.adviceguide.org.uk

The Consumer Credit Association (CCA)

Consumer Credit Association

1 Minerva Court

Minerva Avenue

Chester

CH1 4QT

Telephone: 01244 394760

email: complaints@ccauk.org

Website: www.ccauk.org

Consumer Credit Trade Association (CCTA)

Unit G5, Spring Mill,

Main Street, Wilsden,

West Yorkshire, BD15 0DX

01274 714 959

email: info@ccta.co.uk
Website: www.ccta.co.uk

Finance and Leasing Association (FLA)
15-19 Kingsway
London
WC2B 6JN
020 7836 6511
www.fla.org.uk

Financial Conduct Authority
UK: 0800 111 6768
From abroad: +44 20 7066 1000
www.fca.org.uk
Email: firm.queries@fca.org.uk

Radio, Electrical and Television Retailers Association
Retra Ltd
1st Floor
Woburn Court
2 Railton Road
Woburn Road Industrial Estate
Kempston
Bedford,
MK42 7PN
01234 269110
http://www.retra.co.uk/

Scottish Motor Traders Association

Palmerston House

10 The Loan

South Queensferry

EH30 9NS

0131 331 5510

http://www.smta.co.uk/

Data and Marketing Association

DMA House

70 Margaret Street

London W1W 8SS

020 7291 3300

http://www.dma.org.uk

Citizens Advice Scotland

www.cas.org.uk

0800 028 1456

****

Index

****